GOLDEN THREADS

WOMEN'S SHARED WISDOM FROM THE TAPESTRY OF LIFE

Compiled by Sue Williams

THE BOOK CHIEF®
IGNITE YOUR WRITING

Published by The Book Chief Publishing House 2024
Suite 2A, Blackthorn House, St Paul's Square, Birmingham, B3 1RL
www.thebookchief.com

The moral right of the author has been asserted.

Text Copyright © 2024 by **Sue Williams**

All rights reserved. No part of this book may be reproduced, stored in a retrieval system, or transmitted in any form or by any means, electronic, mechanical, photocopying, recording, public performances or otherwise, without written permission of **Sue Williams**, except for brief quotations embodied in critical articles or reviews. The book is for personal and commercial use and has been agreed by the author.

The right of **Sue Williams** to be identified as the author of this work has been asserted in accordance with sections 77 and 78 of the copyright Designs and Patents Act 1988.

ISBN Number: 978-1-0686981-5-6

Book Cover Design: Deearo Marketing
Editor: Sharon Brown
Formatting / Typesetting: Sharon Brown
Publishing: Sharon Brown

Published by The Book Chief

THE DIVINE TAPESTRY OF LIFE

We are integral strands in this divine tapestry of life

Golden threads of humanity; intricately interwoven,

Entwining vibrant joy with the dull, distant ache of despair;

The heavy heartache of letting go.

Tinged with subtle streaks of sadness,

Stitched through with yearning, allusion of something more:

Magical beyond the realms of pure imagination,

Yet hanging calmly, peaceful, timeless, upon the wall.

Sue Williams

Table of Contents

FOREWORD 7

INTRODUCTION 9

CHAPTER 1 11
    WISDOM WOVEN THROUGH ADVENTURE
        by Bally Binning

CHAPTER 2 21
    THE RELUCTANT GARDENER
        by Carole Donnelly

CHAPTER 3 29
    GOLDEN THREADS OF HOPE BLOWING IN THE WIND
        by Carolyn Parker

CHAPTER 4 37
    THE GOLDEN LIGHT: SOPHIA'S JOURNEY
        by Donna Roberts

CHAPTER 5 47
    BETTY'S JOURNEY – A STORY OF COURAGE AND RESILIENCE
        by Eleanor Sharpe

CHAPTER 6 57
    REFLECTIONS IN THE MIRROR
        by Gillian Routledge

CHAPTER 7 69
    DETERMINED TO FIND THE GOLDEN THREAD
        by Hazel Carter

CHAPTER 8 79
    DELIGHT IN BEING FULLY PRESENT
        by Jean Wolfe

CHAPTER 9 87

   LETTING GO AND GROWING: APPRECIATING THE HARD PARTS
      by LizaMarie Wilson

CHAPTER 10 97

   WISDOM GAINED FROM A WHEELCHAIR AND A THREE-YEAR-OLD
      by Paramjit Oberoi

CHAPTER 11 107

   TO DIAGNOSE OR NOT TO DIAGNOSE? THAT IS THE QUESTION.
      by Pollie Rafferty

CHAPTER 12 115

   MY WONDERFUL LIFE. MY WONDERFUL FUTURE
      by Rachel Hardy

CHAPTER 13 125

   GOLDEN THREADS OF SERENDIPITY
      by Sue Williams

CHAPTER 14 135

   RECLAIMING THE DIVINE FEMININE: MY HEALING JOURNEY FROM ENDOMETRIOSIS
      by Wenke Langhof-Gold

CHAPTER 15 145

   ALWAYS FOLLOW YOUR INTUITION
      by Yasmin Merchant

CONCLUSION 153

CELEBRATION 154

   by Sue Williams *154*

FURTHER BOOKS AND RESOURCES 155

Foreword

by Sharon Brown

I have known Sue Williams for a few years, and if one thing consistently stands out about her, she can weave the most intricate threads of human experience into stories that touch the heart. Sue's compassion, empathy, and insight have always been central to who she is—not only as a writer but as a friend, a guide, and a collector of life's wisdom.

Golden Threads – Women's Shared Wisdom from the Tapestry of Life is not just a collection of stories. It is a testament to the lives of extraordinary women, ordinary in their day-to-day existence but profound in their lived experiences. Under Sue's careful curation, these stories come to life, offering us windows into moments of joy, grief, resilience, and transformation.

What I find most remarkable about this collection is how it encapsulates the essence of Sue herself. She has always believed in the power of connection, vulnerability, and the beauty of sharing our journeys, no matter how difficult. Through her trials and triumphs, she has always sought to lift others, to remind them that they are never truly alone. It is no surprise that this book feels like a conversation with close friends, each story revealing golden threads that bind us together as women and as people.

Much like Sue's own life, these stories are filled with moments of heartache, courage, and hope. They remind us that wisdom is often found in the quietest, most unexpected places. As you turn each page, you will find yourself immersed in the honesty and strength of these women, who share their stories so openly, allowing us to reflect on our own.

To know Sue is to understand the importance of weaving the past, present, and future into a tapestry that celebrates life in all its complexity. This book truly reflects her vision—one that honours the golden threads of wisdom shared between generations through stories, relationships, and the simple act of living fully.

I invite you to explore these stories, take them into your heart, and perhaps, like Sue, find the golden threads that weave through your life.

Introduction

by Sue Williams

The tapestry of each of our lives is inter-woven from so many shared experiences that connect us as women. Yet, throughout history, having a voice and openly sharing these experiences—and the maelstrom of emotions associated with them—has not been easy.

As a member of the baby boomer generation, I am acutely aware of how different circumstances were for my mother and grandmothers. They raised families during a time when societal expectations dictated that careers were secondary – women were expected to leave their jobs once pregnant and step into the role of stay-at-home mothers. I witnessed firsthand the impact this had on my mother, torn between the loss of a career she loved and the expectations on her to raise a family.

While today we enjoy far greater freedoms, many of us still grapple with ancestral patterns, societal expectations, feelings of separation and a lack of self-worth. However, over time, the challenges we overcome and the successes we achieve, enrich our life stories. The golden threads that draw together our experience; strands of hope, adventure, resilience and letting go lead us toward self-awareness and self-acceptance. Such strands form an intricate tapestry portraying our shared healing and wisdom.

It was when I took early retirement from a career in the civil service and embarked on my own journey of healing after my parents died, that I found myself exploring the entrepreneurial world.

In doing so, I was amazed at the inspirational and creative women I met. I felt compelled to help them find their voice and share their stories to improve their self-belief and that of other women.

How often do you pause to reflect on your successes? I passionately believe that, by valuing our unique journeys as women and sharing our hard-won wisdom, we can in turn enrich the lives of other women, empowering them to value themselves and their achievements. This is why I am delighted to present *Golden Threads – Women's Shared Wisdom from the Tapestry of Life,* a collection of true stories that weave together the diverse yet universal experiences of fifteen remarkable women. These women have each lived full lives and join together to generously share the defining moments that have shaped them.

Each author offers examples of strength in vulnerability, courage in adversity, and inspiration for others as they relate their own personal journeys. These women have accepted the call to reflect on their hard-earned wisdom, and to celebrate the turning points they have faced and overcome. Not only that, but their experiences also remind you that you are never alone.

I trust as you dip into the stories in this collection written by "everyday" women, you will discover valuable insights. As you read, I invite you to reflect on your own journey and experiences and to recognise the strands of hard-earned wisdom that run through your own life. May the spirit of honesty, resilience, hope and self-acceptance that weave through these stories encourage you to untangle your own truths, to embrace and celebrate the wisdom that lies within you.

Chapter 1

Wisdom Woven Through Adventure

by Bally Binning

The quaint streets of Leamington Spa seemed to shrink around me as I clutched my TEFL certificate. At 22, I was restless, determined to explore horizons beyond the manicured lawns of Jefferson Gardens.

"Hoor chai?" My mother's voice snapped me back to reality. I was standing in our supermarket, Michael's, the aroma of cardamom and fennel swirling around me.

"Neh, Mom," I replied, my mind already wandering to sun-drenched plazas and bustling foreign markets.

Each day, as I served the same customers, a voice inside me grew louder. It whispered of adventure, making a difference through teaching, and discovering myself in the unfamiliar.

One evening, as I sat looking at people passing by, I made my decision. The air was thick with the whiff of empty vegetable boxes where I sat at the front of the shop—it was a perfect Leamington summer evening out. But for me, it was the eve of a grand adventure.

The Decision

Heart pounding, I gathered my family late one evening. Adorned with faded photos, the walls seemed to close in on me.

A Punjabi song thudded on the telly, a reminder of the cultures that had shaped me.

"I've decided to go overseas to teach English," I blurted out, my voice wavering but determined.

The silence that followed was deafening. My father's brow furrowed, his eyes searching mine for understanding.

"Why?" my father asked, gesturing around the room. His Punjabi accent thickened with emotion. *"You have stability here, a future."*

My mother said, *"You've worked so hard for your TEFL. Surely there are opportunities closer to home? Besides, it's time to get married."*

"I need to do this," I said, surprised by the strength in my voice. *"I need to see the world, to teach, to learn. It's not that I don't value what we have here, but I need to explore beyond Leamington."*

Just then, my phone buzzed. It was Cathy, my new 'TEFL' friend and partner in adventure. *"I've got a contact in Mexico,"* her message read. *"We could have a place to stay. Imagine the stories we'll have!"*

Mexico. The word conjured images of vibrant markets, ancient ruins and endless possibilities. But I knew my parents weren't ready for such a leap.

"I'm thinking of Germany," I lied, hating the deception but seeing it as necessary. *"It's not too far and it's safe."*

The tension in the room eased slightly. My parents exchanged glances, a silent conversation passing between them.

"Promise us you'll stay safe and keep in regular touch," my mother finally said, her eyes glistening.

I hugged them both tightly, feeling their love and concern, even as excitement bubbled within me.

Preparations and Journey

The days that followed were a whirlwind of preparations. Cathy and I discussed our travel plans, practised our rudimentary Spanish, and shopped for essentials.

Our journey began in Los Angeles, our agreed-upon meeting point for a gruelling 48-hour bus ride to Mexico City. As we crossed the border to Tijuana, the landscape shifted dramatically. Cathy's excitement was contagious, and her eyes were wide with wonder at each new sight.

Arriving in Mexico

As we stepped off the bus, Mexico City hit me like a wave. Car horns blared, vendors shouted, and mariachi music played.

"Bienvenidas a México!" Cathy shouted over the noise, her face split by a wide grin.

Our taxi ride to Panticosa, a small neighbourhood in the sprawling metropolis, was a blur of colourful buildings, street art and dizzying traffic. Our new home, a small apartment with peeling paint and a view of a bustling street market, was a shock to the system.

That first week was a sensory overload of new challenges and discoveries; walking to the local market was an adventure.

"Ram-bu-tán," a kind-faced vendor repeated slowly, holding up a strange, hairy red fruit. Her patience with my clumsy Spanish

was touching, a small act of kindness that helped me feel less alone in this vibrant, chaotic world.

The taste of street tacos, the burn of my first sip of mezcal, and the relentless Mexican sun on my skin were all sensations that became opportunities to practice. Even challenges like navigating the crowded metro or deciphering restaurant bills in Spanish became turned into opportunities.

Despite the initial culture shock, Panticosa's charm began to work its magic. Each small victory—successfully ordering a meal or understanding a local joke—felt monumental.

Building Connections

As weeks turned into months, Mexico City became more than just a place – it became a community. At the heart of this transformation were Miguel and Rosa, a couple who took us under their wing with a warmth that felt foreign and familiar.

Miguel, with his artist's soul and twinkling eyes, became my unofficial Spanish tutor. Our lessons often stretched long into the evening, punctuated by laughter and stories.

"Remember, 'ser' is for characteristics that don't change," Miguel explained one evening. *"For example, 'Yo soy profesora' means 'I am a teacher.'"*

"Yo soy profesora," I repeated, tasting the words.

"Perfecto!" he beamed. *"Now, 'estar' is for temporary states. 'Yo estoy cansada' – I am tired."*

"Yo estoy cansada," I echoed, realising with a start that I wasn't just reciting – I truly was tired but in the best possible way.

These language lessons became a metaphor for my broader journey. Each new word and phrase is a step towards understanding Spanish and the culture and people around me.

I met Rosa, Miguel's girlfriend from Philadelphia, at an advertising agency where I trained and she worked. She was a force of nature, and her creative energy and business acumen were in stark contrast to Miguel's laid-back artistry. Through her, I began to see how I might blend my teaching skills with the corporate world—a seed that would later grow into my career as a Performance Coach.

Miguel and Rosa introduced us to a wider circle of friends. Weekend gatherings in Zona Rosa, strung with colourful golden lights and filled with music, became a regular fixture. During one of these parties, I realised how far I'd come from the girl who'd left Leamington Spa.

Surrounded by a mix of locals and fellow expats from around the world, conversation flowed in a blend of Spanish and English. I felt a sense of belonging I hadn't expected to find so far from home.

Looking around at the faces that had become so dear to me, I knew I was changing, growing in ways I couldn't have imagined back in Leamington Spa. Mexico, with its challenges and joys, was shaping me into someone new—someone I was excited to become.

Lessons Learned

The vibrancy of my new life in Mexico made the news of Miguel's death all the more shocking. It came on a Tuesday, a day that had started like any other – the smell of fresh bread from the panadería, the cheerful chaos of the morning market. But by afternoon, our world had shattered.

Rosa's tear-stained face at our door told me everything before she even spoke. *"Miguel,"* she choked out. *"Took his own life."*

The days that followed were a blur of grief and disbelief. The colourful streets of Mexico seemed muted, the joyful sounds of daily life now a discordant noise against our sorrow.

The funeral, held in the historic neighbourhood of Coyoacán, where we'd previously spent evenings together, was a surreal experience. Surrounded by the vibrant colours of Frida Kahlo's old stomping ground, we mourned a man whose artistry had brought so much beauty to the world.

As we stood in the cemetery, I was struck by the community that had gathered. People whose names I didn't know stood shoulder to shoulder with us, united in their love for Miguel. It was a poignant reminder of the connections he had fostered, the lives he had touched.

But even in death, Miguel taught me one final, bitter lesson about the complexities of human nature. As we grappled with our grief, not understanding why he would have done this, supposed family members appeared, more interested in Miguel's valuable artwork than in mourning his loss. Their squabbles over his paintings felt like a desecration of his memory, a harsh reminder that not all connections are built on love and respect.

Rosa and I found solace in each other's company in the following weeks. Our conversations, once filled with laughter and cooking mishaps, now turned to deeper topics—life, death, and the legacy we leave behind.

"Miguel once said life was meant for embracing new beginnings," Rosa told me one evening as we sat in her apartment. The lights, which had once twinkled for joyous

gatherings, now cast a soft, melancholic glow. *"He wouldn't want us to stop living because he's gone."*

Her words struck a chord. I realised that my journey – leaving home, embracing the unknown, forming these profound connections – was exactly what it meant to live fully. Miguel's death, painful as it was, had taught me the value of every moment, every relationship, every experience.

As I dealt with this profound loss so far from home, I found strength I didn't know I possessed. The support of the community Miguel had introduced me to became a lifeline, showing me the power of human connection in the face of adversity.

Reflections and Golden Insights

Returning to Leamington Spa two decades later, that young English teacher who stepped off that bus, wide-eyed and overwhelmed, now serves female leaders as a Performance Coach. I feel like a different person entirely, yet one deeply rooted in the experiences that shaped me.

My roots were a combination of supportive and limiting influences. They provided me with a strong foundation and values, becoming a 'golden thread' guiding me through my adventures. At the same time, the desire to break free from certain expectations drove my personal growth.

Leaving Leamington Spa for Mexico City and eventually returning has helped me appreciate the positive aspects of my upbringing while also recognising the importance of forging my own path.

This journey has taught me more than just a new language or how to navigate a foreign city. It's shown me the true meaning of resilience, the depth of human connection, and the transformative power of stepping out of one's comfort zone.

I've learned that dreams aren't just about personal achievement—they're about growth, about becoming the person you're meant to be. Mexico, with its vibrant culture and warm-hearted people, has shaped me in ways I never anticipated. It's taught me to embrace the unknown, find joy in the every day, and see beauty in diversity.

My relationship with my family, once strained by my decision to leave, has evolved into something stronger and more understanding. They've come to see the value in my journey, and I've learned to appreciate the growth it has provided me.

The skills I honed in Mexico—adaptability, empathy, and cross-cultural communication—have become the foundation of my work as a Performance Coach. Every day, I draw on the lessons learned from Miguel, Rosa, and countless others who touched my life in Mexico.

To anyone standing at the precipice of their own adventure, I say this: take the leap. The unknown may be daunting, but it's where the most profound growth occurs.

Be open to learning, not just through formal means but through every interaction, challenge, and triumph. Let curiosity be your guide and adaptability your strength.

Remember that setbacks are golden opportunities for growth. Each difficulty you overcome is a testament to your resilience. Embrace these moments – they are the true shapers of your character.

Cultivate empathy in all your interactions. Everyone you meet is fighting their own battles, carrying their dreams. A little understanding can bridge the widest cultural gaps and forge the strongest bonds.

Above all, cherish every moment—the joyous ones, certainly, but also the challenging ones. They all contribute to the golden tapestry of your experience, making you stronger, wiser, and more compassionate.

As I look to the future, I'm filled with a sense of excitement and purpose. My journey is far from over—in many ways, it's only just begun. But I carry with me the lessons of Leamington Spa, the vibrancy of Mexico City, and the memory of those who've shaped my path.

Whatever lies ahead, face it with an open heart and adventurous spirit. Life is meant to be lived fully in all its complexity and beauty.

About Bally

Bally Binning is a certified IFC and Performance Coach, MBA and Senior Higher Education Fellow dedicated to empowering mid-level female leaders. With more than 20 years of training background and extensive coaching experience, Bally helps women overcome barriers, achieve their full potential, and create balanced, fulfilling lives through her coaching business, Leaderize.

Bally has been training in AI over the last two years. her business supports individuals wanting to close the AI gap, ensuring they fully utilise emerging technology to drive their success. Her journey exemplifies resilience, community and the pursuit of dreams.

Chapter 2

The Reluctant Gardener

by Carole Donnelly

1: Clearing the way and creating the landscape

When you reach rock bottom, often the only way you can go is up. But what if there is another layer below? I can assure you that there is a hidden layer underneath the hard rock, the molten core that lies beneath it. This is where I found myself in 2019. If the late Queen had her 'annus horribilis' in 1992, this was mine. My world imploded. I walked away from a great job leading a city in the process of developing more social entrepreneurs. I also closed my community business after failing to get the support and funding needed for its survival.

I had burnt out; ignoring the symptoms I had experienced during the previous year:

- Loss of motivation and energy
- Lack of concentration and procrastination
- Irritability and emotional instability
- Negativity and overly critical (of self and others)
- Insomnia and exhaustion

The list seemed endless, and my whole reason for being, had been rocked. I felt I had let everyone down, and the feeling of shame consumed me. I remember feeling so alone as I walked home after locking the community building one last time before handing over the keys. I felt useless, internal pain consuming me like molten rock bubbling beneath the surface of my life. I had a choice: to pick myself up or feel sorry for myself. I chose the latter, as it seemed easier. If a city could abandon me, it would be okay for me to abandon Carole, too.

I spent that summer partying; alcohol was my drug of choice to hide the pain. I threw on a mask, and no one knew. All they saw was the bubbly party girl, not the broken woman. No one noticed the shame I felt. No one asked how I was, and I thought no one cared. This happens when you fall into the molten stuff under rock bottom. It is also when you must act. I am renowned for my bouncebackability, but this time, I would need every ounce of strength I could muster. I had begun the journey back to Carole as we entered 2020, but then COVID-19 struck, and the country shut down!

2: Planting the seeds

For decades, I had been planting seeds of knowledge and nurturing my dreams of what I wanted to achieve. As I entered my 60s in 2020, I fought back and started to build a new business idea and took on a new role two days a week for a housing organisation in Birmingham. In times of stress, we often revert to what we know and where we feel safe. This job was a step back into my comfort zone, but I knew it wasn't what I really wanted to do. When you are at rock bottom, money talks louder than hope, visions and dreams.

Within three weeks of starting that job, the country shut down. Alone and in danger of sinking back into the molten core, I needed a distraction from overthinking, isolation and the fear bubbling inside that *"I wasn't good enough."*

Once the shops re-opened to sell something other than food, I bought paint and revamped the old dull garden furniture in bright, vibrant colours. I started with purple on the table, then bright yellow, blue, turquoise, pink, sea green and orange for the chairs. I didn't stop there; I painted an old butcher's block pink and blue, an old table bright blue and several empty plant pots in bright colours. I was hooked; I had found colour and a purpose in a locked-down, isolated world.

At this point, I noticed a post on Facebook from Smiths Garden Centre. This local nursery had supported my community business for years. I ordered £250 worth of plants. I am no gardener. In 2019, my garden was completely overgrown with forget-me-not plants that had not been cut back. Like my life, it felt overwhelming, and I had no idea where to start. But start I did, digging out borders and planting the plants into the ground. I put others into the pots I'd painted and into baskets alongside my lovely, fresh, rainbow-coloured garden furniture before sitting back and waiting.

The overgrown garden started to transform. As I took time to reflect on what I wanted from life, I revisited a well-being coach who helped me in 2019 to help break the cycle of burnout. I needed to make so many changes. I realised I needed to look after myself better, to put boundaries in place, without knowing how to maintain these changes. The old fears kept cropping up; I was finding it easier to hide and blame a city that had let me down. This is why I share what shame brings to the surface and why the molten layer under rock bottom can consume you.

3: Nurturing and watching the plants bloom

Patience was the main lesson of many that 2020 taught me. Nothing happens in an instant. Growth takes time; the beauty is in this growth and in watching the changes each season. As I began to reflect on how the plants grew and what they needed to flourish, I started applying these concepts in my life. I launched a new consultancy, and this did indeed flourish.

I added a rendered wall, a new fence with rainbow-coloured plant pots attached and multi-coloured lights so the garden glowed at night. The new fence and wall symbolise my new focus on my own personal boundaries and my need to feel secure as I age. I had always wanted a wooden swing where I could sit every day and enjoy the fruits of my labour, so I added a lovely one. I noticed which plants thrived and where to place them. I also noticed which plants struggled to grow in my garden, whether because of the poor soil, the slugs, the lack of rain in the summer of 2022, or the naughty squirrel who ate all my strawberries!

However, as my business grew, I noticed my time spent in the garden dwindled. It was starting to become a chore rather than something that gave me joy. I no longer took time to prune the roses or to cut back the growth of plants that, if left, would revert to their wild roots and take nutrients from more delicate plants. They would steal the sunshine and leave the others to fight for their needs. Many plants hadn't come back by spring, mirroring my internal state.

By April 2023, I recognised the symptoms of burnout again. Continuing to fear famine, I had taken on too much work. Old fears and limiting beliefs were creeping back, taking up space in my brain, just like the weeds in the garden. I noticed my weight increasing, and my wine and poor food choices had crept back, leaving me exhausted and lacking the capacity to be creative for my clients. Like the flowers in my beautiful garden, I had forgotten to nurture myself.

4: A garden needs love and attention

I discovered that the hardest lesson to learn is to look after yourself first. I watched the garden struggle as I left pots empty and didn't nurture the plants or water them daily. Worst of all, I allowed the weeds to overwhelm the colour. I felt the joy my garden had brought me disappearing; it looked sad and neglected, reflecting how I felt. No longer the oasis of calm I had created, by the late summer of 2023, I realised I needed to make massive changes to my beautiful garden and to me too.

Carrying on winning new business to boost my income at the expense of my well-being could no longer be sustainable. I was tired of spending all my time indoors online, in endless meetings and writing reports that, if I'm honest, never got to see the light of day. I decided to focus on myself rather than apply for some new tenders. This upset a few people with whom I would have partnered, but I had put everyone else first for decades. I now recognised that was why I burnt out time and time again, and that was why my garden had become so overgrown and neglected.

After intensive research, I discovered a coaching course focused on health and well-being. It was time for me to use all the skills I had learnt over the last few decades and finally make sense of them. A phrase kept cropping up: *"IF YOU ALWAYS DO WHAT YOU'VE ALWAYS DONE, YOU ALWAYS GET WHAT YOU'VE ALWAYS GOT."* Finally, it started to make sense – the only person getting in my way was me. No one forces me to over-deliver, overwork, eat the wrong food or drink too much wine. I was the one that needed love and attention. My garden had shown me the answer – with the right planning and reading on how to garden, the right plants, good nutrition, and regular watering alongside tender loving care, the garden blooms and looks amazing.

I signed up for a 12-month Health and Well-being Diploma and have since developed my health coaching offer for over 55s. It is time we started putting ourselves first for a change.

5: Maintaining your oasis

Making massive changes to your life takes time and reflection. Thankfully, I have been journalling for the last ten years. When I re-read my journals, I could see the patterns emerge—overwork, overdelivering, and blaming others when, ultimately, I made those choices.

I delved deeper into the health issues that we face as we age. I read many books and spoke with numerous people who were like me. We know what to do, but we don't do it – I needed to understand why.

I progressed with my course, started health coaching and added a trauma-informed course to my toolkit. I gained clarity that, just like with my garden, planning was essential, nutrition was critical, hydration was vital and above all, you don't need to do it alone. Just as it takes time to nurture a garden to life, it takes time to nurture yourself back to full health and to step off the treadmill of burnout. Like me, you will realise we can live a better, more fulfilled and simpler life. We have all spent years planting our seeds of wisdom and need to nurture them.

I may always be a reluctant gardener, but I will never again be a reluctant participant in my self-care and well-being. As I grow my health coaching business, I continue to draw on lessons I learned when I fell into the molten middle and developed strength and character. Consider how a rose bush blooms when nurtured with love, care and attention. Given the right amount of water, sunlight and nutrients, it flourishes with careful pruning and the weeds being kept away.

With similar love, care and attention, you too will bloom as you age well in your golden years.

If my story inspires you, why not join me in the Golden Years Health and Well-being coaching programme to nurture your internal reluctant gardener?

About Carole

Carole Donnelly is an award-winning social entrepreneur who transformed her life in her 60s following burnout. After co-chairing the Social Economy Task Force for the West Midlands Mayor, she added health and well-being coaching to her consultancy. She created the Golden Years Coaching Programme for those over 50s who want to live a great life as they age well. For further details, visit www.cjd.org.uk or email carole@cjd.org.uk CJD Consultancy and Coaching.

Chapter 3

Golden Threads of Hope Blowing in the Wind

by Carolyn Parker

As I reflected on some of the toughest challenges in my life, I made a wondrous discovery: golden threads can be found in the most unexpected and darkest places.

From my unexpected beginnings at an English beach party, my survival and adoption placement in a safe suburban home, through confusion, identity crisis, and the deepest darkness of depression, loneliness, inner rage, turmoil, abuse and utter despair in my forties and fifties – a rope of golden threads has been present. Without it, I would not be here to tell the tale…

I'm aware that when life happens, and I am in the middle of the excitement or the drama of the moment, my perspective becomes warped. I can only see what is in front of my eyes. I react to each new stimulus or situation as it arises. For much of my life, I have jumped from one stepping stone to another without giving myself time to weigh the options and possible consequences. Instead, I move quickly and instinctively, rather than logically, ruled by my fears and need for survival rather than my head.

I felt emotion so keenly in the past. It seemed to consume me. I found it almost impossible at times to reign in the sudden wayward waves of energy coursing through my body, unbidden and untamed. I knew nothing of how energy flows in those days or the different ways we humans are wired. I spent my younger years ignoring it. When powerful negative emotions arose that I didn't understand or found distressing to be with, I would attempt to suppress them, pushing them down in a futile attempt to permanently banish them. I felt mystified about where they originated or how to control them. Emotional intelligence was an alien concept, and I believed I was the only one who struggled with it.

I have since learned that emotions, especially the raw ones, are particularly persistent and can be immensely powerful. Who was I to think I could put them in a box and make them disappear in some Aladdin-like fashion?

Like the tide ebbs and flows, I would be calm one moment before a fierce storm surged through me minutes later, bursting out with a sudden intensity that physically shook me. A verbal torrent of rage would pour from my mouth, scaring me and the victim of my wrath. A few moments later, totally spent, I would fall to the floor in floods of tears. Numb, I would curl into a foetal position, all energy drained from my limbs. Exhausted, confused, silent. Eventually, I consulted my doctor.

"I'm not sure of the cause," he said. *"It could be a few things. I want to run some blood tests and refer you to the psychologist if you are happy to do that, as she has a wider understanding of behavioural patterns than I do."*

On my assessment day, I felt nervous. Would she understand what was happening, I wondered, and what would the outcome be? I needn't have worried. After asking me some basic questions, we agreed to start my sessions by looking at my life timeline. This was my homework before our first session. As I wrote, I recalled a string of emotional traumas, losses, verbal and physical wounds, rejections and misunderstandings (*many misunderstandings*). In each session, we explored these painful times starting in 1959 with my adoption as a baby. I found this process helpful, but something happened just before we reached my teens.

I attended a healing service at my local church one summer Sunday evening. The young preacher spoke passionately, sharing his experiences of God's healing in his life. I listened intently as he relayed the many amazing events he had witnessed. He ended his talk with the words, *"God heals today."* For thirty minutes, I contained my recurring mental comment, *"That's not always true."* Bear in mind that at the time, I was a committed, evangelical Christian who had witnessed, as well as personally experienced, what I can only describe as miraculous healings.

I had bucketloads of faith, but I didn't understand (and couldn't explain) why my eldest daughter hadn't been healed of Asperger's syndrome. Since being diagnosed as on the autistic spectrum, many people, known for their powerful Christian healing ministries, had prayed *with* her, *for* her and *over* her, yet she continued to struggle in her everyday life. If the God I fervently believed in loved my daughter, which my faith told me He did, WHY was she still suffering?

This question is often asked in spiritual communities. One of the most hurtful answers for me is that the sufferer or praying believer has a lack of faith. I have often wondered why religious groups do this, blaming the parents for their child's condition in this way. In my mind, it is cruel and heartless.

I was plunged into the depths of my innermost being that night – a dark place with no answers. I attended the meeting to glean strands of hope and encouragement. Yet, from my emotionally fragile perspective, I received only condemnation. The message I heard was that my daughter hadn't been healed because we lacked faith. As you can imagine, this stung.

Enough was enough. Something had to give. Something had to give *now* ...Release ... Let GO...

"NO!!!!" I screamed, standing up as the preacher closed his Bible. I picked up my chair and threw it towards the front. I was aware of male hands gripping my arms, pinning them behind my back and leading me towards the church hall doorway. My legs seemed to lose their strength. I stumbled forward and collapsed onto the carpet in floods of tears. My arms were loosened, and I curled into my safe child pose, eyes closed, feeling shame wash over me. When I opened them, my friend Ann was kneeling by me, and the congregation had dispersed. The pretence that I was coping well was over. The months of worrying, caring and praying for my daughter, this precious girl I loved *so* dearly, had taken their toll.

If you are a parent like me, you will understand the joy of having a healthy child. No signs of developmental delay were noticed in early childhood. The sudden, unrelenting onset of deterioration in her ability to remember some of the most basic of skills, such as her morning washing and dressing routine, caught everyone by surprise. We trailed around many hospital departments looking for reasons. My expectations of a cure or healing miracle went from buoyancy to feeling battered by the obvious progression of her difficulties. As a concerned mother, I looked everywhere to find some new therapy or treatment. One day, her father and I even drove two hours to London to see a recommended American healer, but sadly, to no avail. Is it any wonder I could not hear the words *"God heals today"* without a surge of despair and frustration?

The day after the church fiasco, I walked around on automatic pilot. I was deeply ashamed. This was a new low. My mind turned to what my church friends may be thinking about me. *"Who is this mad woman, this possessed person we thought we knew?"* they were most likely asking.

Yet more shame wrapped itself around me, fuelling the fire of rage smouldering menacingly beneath the surface. It wasn't long before this molten pool of anger swirling inside erupted again, this time resulting in my voluntary admission to the local open psychiatric hospital. I had no choice. I knew I was out of control. I was out of options. I needed professional help.

I didn't realise this would be the first in a series of events that led to me calling time on my marriage of twenty years. It ended abruptly a few weeks into my stay due to my warped, pessimistic thought patterns at the time. It also temporarily led to my estrangement from both of my daughters. The psychiatric team deemed me to be in an unsafe state of mind, which, though hard to hear (and write), was true at the time. We are still estranged in many respects today.

To protect myself in this alien environment, I wrote Bible verses in felt pen on my arms and legs and spoke out loudly in a strange *"language"* (sounds that came into my head at the moment). This had the desired effect of keeping the other inpatients at a distance from me. As I sat on my single bed looking at my reflection in the window pane, I realised I didn't know or even recognise myself anymore.

Yet even in this deep, dense darkness, I can now see a few golden threads blowing in the wind. You may have thought one of these was the understanding, supportive mental health care team around me, but sadly, you would be wrong. However, amidst the tedious daily nothingness of the unit, I rediscovered my childhood love for drawing in the weekly art therapy session. This was the only intervention that touched the spot and saved me from my suicidal tendencies.

I quickly filled several A3 sketchbooks with imagery inspired by the music CDs I had brought into the unit. I listened to them on repeat throughout the day for comfort. Most afternoons, you would find me sitting at my desk, headphones on, singing songs from Westlife, The Lighthouse Family or Take That. This was my new happy place, a bubble of pure contentment. I enjoyed the feel of my drawing pens and coloured pencils flying across the page in time to the tunes. Each day, I would choose the title or a short phrase from the lyrics of a track on my chosen album. I would write it at the top of a fresh blank page of my sketch pad before illustrating it with images that appeared in my mind's eye as the tunes danced through my brain.

If you had watched me through the small side window, you may have seen a smile slowly spread across my face as the tunes began to play and the lines on my brow softened. You may have noticed my shoulders drop and a change in the pattern of the rise and fall of my chest as I took a deeper breath in before singing out the following line of the song. Finally, I had found a doorway to peace after many months of anxiety and depression.

The music was the second golden thread that wound its magic around me in those precious moments of creativity. It soothed my troubled soul. It reassured me that all was well in this special, safe space of relative sanity I'd carved out amid the mental maelstrom that swirled around me.

A third strand of glorious golden goodness was also present, which I have often taken for granted. I quietly reflected on what I wanted to say in this short chapter and visualised a beautiful picture. A road with twists represented my life and turns snaking into the distance to the day of my birth and beyond. As I looked, it appeared to be running right through my body, representing my future moments, days and years.

Along this wandering road were words representing experiences, some exciting, some excruciating and some in between. I then noticed a name, sometimes several, inscribed in gold by the side of each challenging moment. These names were those golden ones who had sheltered, supported and been there for me, believing in me when I was staggering through the worst of times, places and inner turmoil on my journey.

I will be eternally grateful to them, for without them, I may not have survived to reach the better and more beautiful life I live now.

About Carolyn

Carolyn Parker is from rural Leicestershire and describes herself as a "*people person.*" Now in midlife, she has a colourful back catalogue of stories to inform her writing.

"*From A Place Called Shame*" – Carolyn's debut memoir of love, life and loss (2022) explores her challenges in adolescence and motherhood. '*Finding Little Me – Learning to Love and Live with My Inner Child*" (2024) followed. Carolyn is a contributor to several inspirational collaborative books. You can find out more about Carolyn and her books at

https://www.carolynparkerauthor.co.uk.

Chapter 4

The Golden Light: Sophia's Journey

by Donna Roberts

As you embark on this journey with Sophia, I invite you to open your heart and mind to the wonders of synchronicity and inner wisdom. My own real-life encounters inspire her experiences with the mystical and the unseen threads that guide us.

My name is Donna Roberts. Throughout my life, I have been blessed with moments that transcend the ordinary, revealing the profound interconnectedness of all things. These experiences have shaped my understanding of the world, leading me to embrace a path of spiritual exploration and personal growth.

May Sophia's journey remind you of the magic in everyday life and inspire you to listen to your inner wisdom and trust the guidance that comes from within.

Switch off your phone and any other distractions, including your thinking mind. Are you sitting comfortably? Let's begin. Take a nice deep breath. As you exhale, become aware of how the breath moves the body. Follow the breath as you feel your shoulders rise and fall, the breath moving in and out through the nostrils, and how your chest rises and relaxes with each inhalation and exhalation. Allow yourself to relax deeply now, breathing in and out without thought. Let your focus remain inward with the breath, engaging your imagination now. In this relaxed state, let me tell you the story of Sophia, who invites you to embark on a beautiful inner journey.

One morning, Sophia woke with vivid memories of a dream that felt remarkably real. In the dream, she encountered an olive-skinned woman with long, glossy black hair adorned with a headdress that fanned out like peacock feathers, symbolising wisdom and beauty. The woman's attire echoed ancient traditions. Around her neck, she wore a gold necklace decorated with red beads and turquoise crystals. She stood barefoot upon a grey, weathered stone plinth, arms raised in a V shape, before a stunning vista of lush green mountains. She called to the elements, reciting a sacred prayer to the Cosmic Mother and Earth Mother. The air around her shimmered as she spoke. Sophia sensed a powerful message: a vortex had opened, bringing the Golden Light of the Divine to Earth. The dream felt like a calling, a reminder of a connection that transcended time and space. The day passed; the dream faded from her memory, tucked away in the recesses of her heart and mind.

Years went by, filled with the routines of daily life. One day, Sophia's father called her. *"Sophia, I have something special for you,"* he said as he handed her a wrapped package. *"It's a book about ancient wonders of the world. I thought you might find it interesting."* *"Thank you, Dad!"* Sophia replied, her eyes alight with curiosity. *"I can't wait to read it."*

As Sophia excitedly turned the pages, a picture jumped out— she'd seen it before! It was of the same lush green mountain range and even the grey, weathered plinth the woman had stood upon. The dream flooded back. Sophia realised it was a real place. Curious to discover more, she flicked through the pages and discovered the pictures were of Machu Picchu, Peru.

The vivid dream with its powerful message, the lush green mountain range, and her father's gift of the book were like pieces of a puzzle being woven together, leading her on a quest.

For years, Sophia imagined travelling to Peru, gathering information just in case. Life continued; she finished school, started work, had children, and moved home several times.

Recollections of mystical moments throughout her life began to flash before Sophia. One was when she strolled through a field of wildflowers. Sophia's attention was drawn to a single red poppy that stood out amongst the rest. This poppy appeared luminous. Sophia could see its petals almost glowing with an inner light against the backdrop of green. It swayed and danced in the breeze as if joyfully acknowledging Sophia's presence.

"This is more than just a flower," she thought. *"It's like it's alive with a message for me. Am I imagining this? No, it feels too real, too vibrant. What is it trying to tell me?"*

Sophia was flooded with an unexpected sensation. The poppy seemed to communicate with her telepathically, as if it had a voice, exuberantly greeting her: *"Hello! Hi! Look at me! I'm so happy you can see me!"*

Inspired by her encounter with the poppy, Sophia found herself increasingly drawn to nature. On another occasion, she ventured deep into the forest with a friend, seeking a quiet meditation spot. *"Can you watch out for passers-by while I meditate?"* Sophia requested as they settled into a serene, secluded place.

"Of course, take your time," her friend replied, settling down with a book. Sophia closed her eyes, tuning into her inner senses. She focused on her breath, inhaling and exhaling slowly, each

breath drawing her deeper and deeper into a state of profound relaxation. She began to feel her surroundings with heightened awareness: "*I need this connection,*" she thought. *"I need to feel unity with nature again. Can I sense the sounds and energy around me, as I recall doing as a child?"*

Sophia's inner voice emerged in this tranquil state, gently guiding her:*' Can you feel the sound of the water cascading into the river? Can you feel the melody of the birds singing? Can you sense the rustling of the leaves as the breeze whispers through the trees?'* Each inquiry deepened her connection to the natural world, blurring the boundaries between her physical form and the vibrant energy around her. Sophia felt an overwhelming sense of expansion and peace as if she had become part of the very essence of the forest. *"WOW,"* she whispered in awe, her eyes wide open, as she witnessed a sea of vibrating energy around her. Everything, including the trees, the ground, and even the air itself, was encompassed by this vibration, a living, pulsating energy.

In this heightened state of awareness, a message resonated within her:

'FEEL, SEE and THINK with your HEART. What you are experiencing now is always present, surrounding you, within you, and throughout everything. All is One.'

The vision of the sea of energy reminded Sophia that the physical world is but a thin veil over a vast, interconnected web of life. She felt a profound sense of connection, a deep knowing that she was an integral part of this endless dance of energy, connecting everything and everybody as ONE.

The profound experiences in the woods lingered in Sophia's mind, deepening her connection to the natural world. During this period of heightened awareness, a friend shared his interest in Shamanism and an intriguing drawing he had sketched depicting a Shaman seen in his dream. Shortly after, Sophia saw a social media post about a journey to the Amazon Rainforest. Thinking of her friend, his dream and the drawing, she forwarded it to him. However, he wasn't interested, so the trip facilitator reached out to Sophia and invited her to join, although no dates had yet been confirmed.

Sophia wasn't well travelled; only package holidays with family, and had yet to even consider the trip for herself, as a lone traveller. More importantly, how would the costs be covered? Memories arose of her own dream of the woman and the lush green mountain range. *'This is so out of my comfort zone,'* Sophia thought, *'but I feel this undeniable pull. It's as if something greater is guiding me. Can I really trust this process? Will everything fall into place?'*

Sophia felt she was not alone. She could only describe being accompanied by a powerful tsunami of energy flowing within her. *'I have to sit back and allow the current to take me',* Sophia thought. The whole experience was fascinating.

Speaking with the trip facilitator, Sophia said she would need a travel angel to arrange everything. The trip facilitator shared her experience from three months prior. Sitting on a beach in Spain, she was inwardly told to arrange an authentic healing experience with the Shipibo Shamans of the Amazon Rainforest at an affordable price and that the right people would come!

Once the initial excitement of planning the trip subsided, practical concerns began to surface. The trip facilitator and Sophia connected by video call to discuss the logistics. "*I've never done anything like this before,*" Sophia admitted, "*I don't* even know where to start or where the funding for the trip will come from."

"Don't worry," the facilitator reassured her, *"I'll help you with everything. Just trust the process."*

Sophia returned to work and could feel the powerful tsunami of energy with her. A colleague unexpectedly and assertively approached Sophia, urging her to claim PPI compensation. *"What?"* Sophia had no idea what he was talking about. Yet, she knew she needed to listen by the tone and manner he had spoken to her. Sophia was in a state of confusion.

'*Why would he blurt this information out to me?*' Sophia thought. With urgency in his voice, he continued to tell Sophia, *"I applied and received thousands in compensation; you need to do it now."* He emailed the forms to Sophia. Acting swiftly, Sophia completed the paperwork, realising she needed an envelope and stamp.

Simultaneously, she sensed the tsunami of energy within her. In her inner vision, she could see a large white A5 envelope. Sophia knew her employer only used buff pre-paid envelopes. Feeling playful, she opened the door to the stationery room, knowing there would be an A5 white envelope. Right in front of her on the shelf was a big box of A5 white envelopes! Laughing at the synchronicities playing out, Sophia decided to test things further.

'*Now for manifesting a stamp!*' Sophia thought. Instantly, she received: '*Ask Janet now!*'

"Excuse me, do you have a first-class stamp I can buy?" Sophia asked, interrupting Janet. *"Sure, let me get one for you,"* Janet replied, immediately stopping her work. *"No need to pay me back."*

The documents, envelope and stamp were all completed; the post box and Royal Mail depot were opposite her workplace. Contemplating which exit to use, Sophia became rooted to the spot, suspended in time. Inwardly, she heard: *'STOP! Breathe, feel your feet on the ground, and be here and now.'*

'OK, I'm here,' Sophia answered, then heard, *'Go to the back door now.'*

Feeling her feet release, Sophia's body steered her left towards the rear staff entrance. The doorbell rang as she reached the door. Can you guess who it was? The Royal Mail courier clutching a grey mail sack. He held out his hand: *"Oh, hello, is that for me? Thank you"*

"This letter is important; can you ensure it arrives safely?" Sophia asked. *"That's my job,"* he replied, smiling and taking the envelope from Sophia. Sophia stood in silent awe at what had unfolded.

Miraculously, everything Sophia needed for her trip appeared. An unexpected windfall from the PPI compensation claim covered the cost of the entire trip. Sophia's dream of the Amazon suddenly came alive. Her travel angel had been divinely sent and informed Sophia she would arrange everything. True to her word, she did. The flights were booked for December 2012, marking the continuation of Sophia's extraordinary adventure – immersing herself in the ceremonies of the Shipibo Shamans in the heart of the Amazon Rainforest.

Sophia's journey is one of many synchronicities she encounters along the way. None are fiction, but a reflection of the incredible wisdom, guidance, and a glimpse of the experiences I have received in my own life. True magic unfolds in the moments we remain present, listening, and trusting in the flow of life. Every encounter is a thread woven, whether perceived as good, bad, or indifferent, into the tapestry of our own life story, a continuum of endless beginnings and transformations.

Life is always present; one may ask oneself, "AM I?"

Etymonline – Online Etymology Dictionary

*Sophia – fem.

The proper name, from the Greek Sophia, means *"skill, knowledge of, acquaintance with; sound judgement, practical wisdom; cunning, shrewdness; philosophy,"* also *"wisdom personified."*

About Donna

Donna Roberts is based in Staffordshire, UK. She is a Public Servant, Skills Coach, trained Holistic Therapist, and co-author of *"Art Peace,"* a Mindfulness Meditation Colouring Book for Creative Minds. From a young age, she has been blessed with moments that transcend the ordinary. These experiences have shaped her understanding of the world, leading her to embrace a path of spiritual exploration and personal growth.

Chapter 5

Betty's Journey – A Story of Courage and Resilience

by Eleanor Sharpe

Close your eyes and imagine the sound of screeching tyres...that is how I felt when I was told I had stage 2 breast cancer. *"Will I die?"* swiftly followed by, *"I am going to have to tell everyone."*

On the morning of 17 January 2024, I was due to attend a mammogram.

I felt a little anxious about attending this appointment because I had been experiencing some pain in my left side for a few weeks. I have benign cysts in both breasts, which can be caused by something harmless, but I was looking forward to my mind being put at rest.

When I got home, I told my husband Ian, *"it all seemed very straightforward."*

On 27 January, I received a letter from Kings' College Hospital in London. The letter stated that my recent mammogram resulted in the need for further investigation. *"It may be a non-cancerous issue... You might want to bring somebody with you."*

I had begun to meet with Jean Branch, a holistic healer, not appreciating how significant that would become... healing is a core part of recovery from illness. I told friends that I had a recall. They reassured me that it was nothing to worry about.

At the hospital on Thursday, 1 February, Ian and I were taken to a dark but overheated consulting room, where I felt an immediate sweat break out. We were swiftly met by a jolly nurse who said in a lovely Irish lilt, *"you look so well, I'm sure you will be fine."* I clung to these words as I underwent a further mammogram.

Back in the consulting room, fully dressed again but feeling shivery with fear, our attention was drawn to a small white blob on the screen on my left side. *"It concerns me that it is pulling away to one side; this could indicate a 'radial scar', which is non-cancerous. I need to be sure. Can you stay for a biopsy?"*

Feeling confused, I followed the nurse to the icy cold biopsy room.

Climbing onto a large bed, I was asked to dangle my left breast through a hole while I faced downward. My breast was injected to numb the area, which felt like a hot piercing needle, enabling the consultant to insert a clip where the tumour may be located.

I could hear the nurse discuss my symptoms with the Consultant. *"The cancer may have spread beyond her lymph nodes"*, he replied. My hopes were crushed.

I had read that swift results may mean the issue was uncomplicated unless the multidisciplinary team agree to meet to discuss a treatment plan. I was informed that my results would be back on 13 February. 'That's ten days of waiting,' I thought with horror.

"My anxiety levels are through the roof," I said to Ian.

Diagnosis

"Sorry..." kind but factual. *"We have found cancer to be present, an invasive ductal carcinoma in situ (DCIS), a type of breast cancer that starts in the milk ducts and may spread to other parts of the body via the lymph nodes."*

"I am going to cry," was all I could utter, to which the kind consultant replied, *"It's okay. It's treatable, and we will look after you for five years."* *"Thank you,"* I said weakly. *"Are you free on Wednesday, 28 February, for surgery"*?

Feeling hugely vulnerable, the words 'stage 2 breast cancer' echoed in my mind, sending it whirring with thoughts of what this meant.

I became aware that the breast cancer nurse had appeared in the room. Ian and I followed her quietly to where she handed me a range of literature produced by the wonderful charity Breast Cancer Now ... looking back, Breast Cancer Now has been endlessly helpful, but then I felt very muddled. *"How much time will I need off work? I can't compute all of this"* was all I could manage. *"Take this pack home and read it slowly. Stop looking up Dr. Google; the literature will become your bible,"* she said kindly.

Can you imagine having two weeks to cancel your life?

Cancelling a holiday, gym membership, socials, theatre trips, handing my job over and pulling out of key work projects. What broke my heart, however, was leaving my beloved rock choir with all the lovely friendships fostered over twelve years of membership, knowing I would not return fully for a while.

"Yippee!" My pre-op would be the very next day, and it felt oddly exciting to have a diary appointment among all the cancellations.

I first shared the news with my Step Mum and Dad, of advanced years, which was particularly sad. I wrote a round-robin message to all my WhatsApp contacts. As kind responses flooded in, I remember thinking I would need to rely on my strength and resources. Nobody can be with you when you enter an operating theatre or undergo a CT scan.

I read everything that I could about breast cancer, so long as it was a trusted source – this is important because there is a huge amount of misinformation out there. When I woke up at 2 am, knowing I could reach out to the Breast Cancer Now website for a symptom check was reassuring.

I decided to give my problem an identity. I called her *"Betty."* I could provide regular updates to friends on Betty's adventures. It helped to take ownership of the issue and add a bit of fun to something that was obviously frightening.

On surgery day, nil by mouth for eight hours, I managed to put my gown and surgical socks on the wrong way around, which the nurse and I laughed about! The anaesthetist popped the canular into my hand. *"I'm about to give you a legal high; not bad for 10 am"*.

Back home, sore and tired, I had an immediate sense of identity loss as the breast looked and felt different. I thought of my cancer as an unwanted intruder, now removed, but I must rid myself of the baggage it left behind.

I was overwhelmed with cards and gifts. The feeling of love was incredibly special, and it is something I will hold dear for the rest of my life. I was also exhausted and emotional, and when my breast cancer nurse called me around two weeks later, I just cried with relief. The isolation and anxiety of waiting for results is quite unbearable.

I recall going to the cinema to watch the Bob Marley biopic, and all the way home, I sang to myself, *"don't worry about a thing, cos every little thing gonna be alright."* What a mantra! That evening, I sat on the stairs and sobbed in Ian's arms. It all felt so unfair!

On 7 March, we met with the consultant. As we entered his consulting room, I heard, *"Eleanor, whenever you come into my office, you take your top off!"*

Next, he delivered the amazing news. *"We removed the tumour successfully. You have clear margins."* All cancer patients want to hear the words *"clear."* My cancer had not spread. Beyond relieved but not knowing how to feel, I hung onto his words. *"Your cancer journey is not quite over, but my advice is – enjoy your life."*

Oncology and radiotherapy

On 5 April, we met with the Oncologist; my prognosis was described as *"good"*. However, should the cancer return, my breast would need to *"come off."* Very blunt. As my diagnosis was oestrogen positive (EP), I was given the drug letrozole along with another drug and calcium to take for the next five years.

Radiotherapy began in late April, but because the issue was on my left side, I would need to protect my heart with deep breaths inspirational holds. This requires holding your breath through the diaphragm for 30 seconds whilst radiotherapy is delivered. Harder than you think! I felt sore and fatigued for a while post-treatment.

I learned that the effect of radiology is that the skin becomes scar tissue, and I will need to avoid sunbathing in the area for at least one year. I still struggle to touch my skin at times, as it is super sensitive.

Life post-treatment and learnings

I am beyond grateful. I believe I have always been a grateful person. Still, the harsh reality of a cancer diagnosis and facing a care team of more than 30 people, all intent on preserving your life, is very humbling.

Cancer is not just life-threatening; it's life-changing...it has left me with a permanent mental scar because treatment is intense, traumatic and often very quick. I am blessed to have Jean, my holistic healer, to support me with rebuilding confidence and my fantastic husband, without whom I could not have come through it all.

Some friends were keener to know more than others. Navigating my way through those people's responses was as difficult as dealing with the diagnosis itself. Even if you find yourself struggling with the news of a friend's diagnosis, try and ensure you offer them some form of support.

Cancer is scary, and most people are afraid of it. Nobody means to be unkind, but inevitably, sometimes people will say the wrong thing. People would tell me I was lucky. Lucky it was only in the early stages, lucky it had been caught early, lucky I didn't need chemo, and lucky I had a good employer and a lovely husband. Although not untrue, I certainly didn't feel lucky. Lucky for me is about having good health.

Try to avoid telling a cancer patient to *"battle"* their disease. This can feel like defeat.

A common question I get asked is: *"Did you know you had cancer?"* Symptoms can sometimes present early, but cancer is likely to cause discomfort in the later stages of the disease.

When I was first diagnosed, I felt responsible, assuming it was my fault. This weighed very heavily on me for a while until I understood that cancer is a genetic disease caused by changes to the genes that control the way our cells function, especially how they grow and divide.

Breasts are a part of a woman's identity. My cancer diagnosis felt like grieving. Loss of health, independence for a time, feeling female, feeling youthful, and losing control. Jean helped me to set an intention around my illness: *"I believe in my own body's ability to heal."* This phrase will stay with me forever.

I loved receiving cards, then phone calls and general offers of support from friends. I can recall meeting with my rock choir friends for coffee post-surgery, and they handed me a glorious bag of thoughtful goodies. I burst into tears.

Many people have referred to me as positive and brave. My official title is Breast Cancer Survivor, but survival is not just about treatment. I do need to keep a positive attitude, as I won't be in remission for five years. Each day is a testament to my resilience and human spirit as I move forward. I've learned to cherish every moment, nurture my body and soul, and support others facing similar battles. I regard my scars as symbols of strength and survival.

I have learned to appreciate each day.

Moving forwards

Bravely, I attended the Breast Cancer Now *"Moving Forwards"* course to meet with primary breast cancer survivors. We remain in contact, which has been invaluable because it has helped reduce the isolation, fear of the future and worry over possible recurrence.

During treatment, some of my friends described my illness as being *"similar to Covid."* I could understand this from an isolation point of view, but sitting and waiting for each day to pass to the next appointment really cannot compare. I suffered anxiety throughout this time.

When treatment finishes, does everything go back to normal?

I am a changed person because I view my life more immediately. I take each day as it comes and do not sweat the small stuff. What matters now is my health and happiness.

My illness has made me more focused on self-care and a little less tolerant of negativity. I have learned to love my warrior scars!

About Eleanor

Eleanor Sharpe is a Civil Service PA who lives with her husband, Ian, and their cat, Missy, in Southeast London. She loves singing with the Rock Choir, exercise, theatre, and rock and pop concerts. Eleanor was unable to have children but was fortunate to make friends through a group she met during and after her fertility treatment. One of her friends is another co-author, Hazel Carter.

Rockchoir.com

References

Cancer Research UK

Breast cancer is now the most common cancer in the UK.

1 in 7 women in the UK develop breast cancer during their lifetime.

Digital.NHS.UK

In 2022, 35.4% of women did not attend their appointments following an invitation, increasing to 46.3% of women being invited for the first time.

Jean Branch

Homeopathy and Nutritional advice for Southeast London - Homeopath for Greenwich and Lewisham (branchhealth.com)

Breast Cancer Now

Breast Cancer Now | The research and support charity

Chapter 6

Reflections in the Mirror
My Story – A Journey of Transformation

by Gillian Routledge

Our lives are connected by numerous golden threads that weave our journey from past experiences to future relationships. These threads shape who we are and who we attract into our lives. Before sharing my story of transformation, let me reflect on some questions that highlight common issues we face in significant relationships. These reflections are crucial for recognising and letting go of old patterns, making different choices, and creating change, ultimately leading to healthier relationships with ourselves and others.

Reflections in the mirror:

Questions to ponder:

- Do you feel caught in a cycle of repetitive patterns in your relationships?
- Do you feel controlled?
- Are you constantly doing things for others?
- Do you feel lost or alone?
- Do you find it difficult to voice your needs?
- Do you feel trapped in a life that doesn't feel like it belongs to you?

The topics in these questions reflect my own experiences, and I would like to share how it all changed for me, offering you guidance to improve your relationships.

My Story – a Journey of Transformation

A friend commented recently that she noticed a beautiful energy between my husband and me; it was obvious he adores me. However, it hasn't always felt this way. For many years, I struggled with feeling unloved, unsupported, and invalidated.

So, what changed? How did our relationship turn around? As a coach and therapist, when working with couples I help to repair the fragmented relationships that can be a result of a breakdown in communication.

Before elaborating on transitioning from a failing relationship to a fulfilling one, I would love to share my story to illustrate the mystery of the golden threads that connect us to our loved ones.

A Turning Point

I'm sitting next to him, yet we may as well be on different continents. I'm staring out of the window at unfamiliar territory. The incessant mundane chatter of strangers on the bus hums in my ears. I feel the anxiety building in my gut like a hard cricket ball. Wherever we are, it doesn't feel right. Fear floods every fibre of my being, telling me we are heading in the wrong direction. I turn to express my concern to my husband; *"Do you know where we are heading? It feels like the wrong direction."* He avoids eye contact and replies dismissively, *"It's fine; treat it as an adventure."*

I feel controlled and frustrated. Inwardly, I know it's not fine as we continue through the suburbs of Sydney. Am I overreacting, or am I within my rights to question his authority? I feel I could jump off the bus, but I stop myself, having no idea how to get back if I did.

This scenario was emblematic of my inner turmoil and the challenges in my relationship. Feeling out of control and wanting to escape was a common theme in my life.

Have you ever felt like running away but know it is not the answer? I felt like this for many years, packing my bags with the intention of leaving. Yet, I often felt stuck when choosing between staying with my husband or moving in with my mother. Even short visits with her, well-intentioned as she was, rarely worked. Perhaps you relate to my feeling of being stuck between what I would call a rock and a hard place.

The rational me knew that running was not an option; an invisible cord seemed to keep us tied together. There was something I needed to address and had not fathomed out. The real challenge I faced was unresolved issues from the past. My current need to run resulted from a tenuous link with a past trauma. Looking back, it was a repetition of numerous scenarios where I didn't have the right to speak out. Not speaking my truth caused a sense of resignation, like something was dying inside. The feelings present in my body were those of a small child, showing me something from my past that required healing. Forgiveness of others and self-forgiveness became crucial steps in my healing journey.

Navigating Relationship Complexities

Relationships are inherently complex. Common issues, such as blame, frustration, feeling trapped, lack of communication or misinterpretation, often arise. I have learned that the key to transformation is awareness and conscious choice. Instead of continually blaming my husband or expecting him to change, I changed my responses and actions. Here are some of the practices that helped me:

Journaling and Awareness

Writing and journaling became a daily practice and continue to help me build more awareness of what I can change. This also enables me to express frustrations on paper without taking them out on others. I also found other tools, such as Neuro-Linguistic Programming (NLP), which became a regular practice to break down my old beliefs. Small steps over time eventually led to dramatic change overall.

The following is a simple three-step process I recommend to recognise old beliefs and replace them with positive choices:

The A B C of Transformation

A is for Awareness

Recognise how you respond during conflicts in your relationships. Awareness empowers change. Rather than focusing on the other person or wanting to fix them, become more aware of your part in conflicting situations. The other person may be acting as a mirror for traits you dislike within yourself. When we change, often others around us change too.

B is for Belief – Busting Old Beliefs and Building Self-Belief

Sometimes, we hold onto old beliefs that negatively impact our relationships. Some we are aware of, others we can be blind to. Do you find yourself saying phrases like: *"He will never change," "He will always do this or be like that."* This is a sign that you are caught up in a negative cycle of beliefs that ensure nothing will change. The answer is to challenge those negative beliefs which hinder our relationships. When we question the validity of our beliefs, we ask, *"Is that true?"* By doing so, we can break down the barriers keeping us stuck.

C is for Conscious Choices – Choosing Healthier Patterns of Behaviour

Making deliberate choices is the way to adopt healthier behaviours. How do you make more conscious choices? Start with small, simple steps, as over time, these can lead to significant changes. For example, if blaming is a habit you want to change, begin by bringing awareness to when this behaviour occurs. Next, examine any beliefs you may have about this. It could be a pattern you witnessed in childhood.

Growing up, I became a sounding board for my mother's complaints about my father. She avoided confronting him due to fear of conflict, sometimes leaving because she couldn't cope. In my own relationship with my husband, I adopted these tendencies as a learned response. It has taken years of therapy to let go of these inherited habits, fears, and beliefs that were not even mine.

Choose to cut the cords to that inherited pattern and notice what changes. Forgiving the people or situations from the past is fundamental to healing.

Reflections of you

The poem below highlights the reflective process of seeing my tendencies mirrored in my husband's reaction. It underlines the importance of self-awareness and inner work.

Reflections of you

*What do I see
is it you, or is it me
Traits of who I am could be
or should be.
Sometimes liked
sometimes abhorred.
Choices to contemplate
sometimes ignored.
Old patterns in me
reflected as you.
What can be done
what should I do?
Temptation to blame
to scream to the world
this isn't me.
Looking to run
to escape to be free
from the you that I see as me.
Look deeper and beyond the glass screen
of the behaviours and patterns
we've been.
Dive into the core
the fathomless unseen.
What is in the depths of the you and me
free from the traps and masks of who
we should be.
The truth of being and loving
unconditionally.*

You might like to journal about the feelings the poem evokes or write a poem that captures how reflections are playing out in your relationship. I have found that this can be a very therapeutic process.

Back on that bus in Australia, facing the old demons of blaming and shaming, I asked myself a simple question in response to my husband's behaviour: *"When have you done this?"* Reflecting on my response to this question halted the pattern playing out, allowing me to witness and sit with my emotions until they had run their course.

I realised my husband is not the enemy. In my subconscious, a scared child equated fear to not being safe. This underlines the importance of looking within and seeking to change how we respond and react in challenging situations. As I changed, my relationship with my husband improved. I recognised that my fear was illogical and out of proportion to my situation.

This awareness opened a new opportunity to self-process. Self-processing involves sitting in the core of the emotion, dropping through all the layers of the emotions that arise until they have passed through you. I gained this wisdom by asking myself that one simple question and sitting with the response on the bus that day.

Golden Threads: The Awaken to Love Method

There are golden threads that weave through relationships, whether with ourselves, our loved ones, or both. The following simple guidelines, which I use as part of my six-step programme, 'The Awaken to Love' method, are developed from my own experience and learnings over many years.

Golden Threads:

T – Time to be present
H – Heal the past
R – Release the tendency to blame others
E – Experience each moment as a gift
A – Accept and Allow (Ask a different question)
D – Divorce from old patterns and behaviours
S – Simplify and live

I have been asked to write a book about this process, so watch this space for more!

Embracing the Present

Reflecting on the past and learning from it is the crucial first element of my process. While the past shapes our future, it doesn't have to define it. When we are willing to learn, adapt, and change old patterns that have kept us stuck in the past, we are free to live a more fulfilling life in all areas—relationships, work, community, or finances. Once more, I have expressed this creatively in a poem.

Past and Present

You say the past is the past, yet it prods us and pokes us
To remind us today that the hurts and the pains
Have not gone away
The patterns of blaming and shaming
Partners and parents
distract come what may
Yet till we reflect and responsibly
Own our part we will
Remain in dismay
Learning to love

To forgive and let live
Simply in tune with our purpose
To give and receive
Living in love
Is a present
till the end of the day.

This poem illustrates how the life we have been given is a precious gift. We are all unique. Each of us has a part to play and a purpose to be rediscovered. Why do I say rediscovered? We all inherently know our purpose, but it can become obscured as life distracts us. We are conditioned to be sensible, grow up, be responsible and find a regular job to pay the bills. Yet, we are each significant.

We can make a difference in the world, in our world, with those whose lives we touch. We come into this world as innocent babes with no judgment, yet we learn behaviours such as judging and blaming passed down through the generations. By becoming more aware and intentional, we can find ways to unlearn the unhealthy tendencies and behaviours that have often kept us stuck for many years.

When we catch ourselves in judgment and make a different choice, we can let go of the old pattern that keeps us stuck in the past and cut the ties to that old cycle, creating a new paradigm for our future.

Listening to our inner guidance with discernment helps us differentiate between ego and truth, leading to healthier relationships. As we appreciate everything we are, recognise that we were born to be magnificent, powerful, and creative, and see these qualities in others, we foster a healthier, more loving community. This self-awareness and transformation process is lifelong but worth taking. The invitation is to take each step towards a more loving and fulfilling life as it appears and treat every situation and interaction as a gift.

About Gillian

Gillian is an author, speaker, and guide on the transformative journey 'Discovering the Love Within.' Founder of the Awaken to Love method, she helps conflicted couples fall in love again. Her personal story serves as a testament to her commitment to helping others reconnect with love in its purest form. She shares her own trials in life, offering solace and relatability to those facing similar challenges.

Gillian offers talks and programs tailored for individuals, couples and groups. www.gillianroutledge.com

Chapter 7

Determined to Find the Golden Thread

by Hazel Carter

Reflecting on your life to find the common thread that defines you is enlightening. For me, this golden thread is woven with strands of resilience, determination and love.

People see me as a strong, confident, successful woman. They might assume I had a happy childhood and graduated from university. But my life has been a tapestry of challenges I have met with determination and resilience.

If people knew the truth, they would realise I am battle-scarred and would wonder why I am not completely broken.

Early life

Moving from beautiful North Devon to a small, dark cottage in Birmingham at age five marked the beginning of a challenging childhood characterised by scarcity and conflict. I cried often; the long journey and the busy road outside our new home filled me with fear.

Dad worked as a labourer at the local farm. *"Your dad has a quick temper,"* Mum, a fiery redhead, would say. Without enough money or food, they rowed a lot. Often, I arrived home from school to hear Dad say, *"Your mum's left us again and taken your brother and sister."* The bread and jam we ate until she returned stuck in my throat as I held back my tears.

Smarting from the belt used to discipline me, I wept in the outhouse toilet while our dog licked my tears. I cried harder the day he got run over. Feeling unloved, I daydreamed about running away to play with my cousins on the beach in Devon.

By age ten, we'd moved to a council house, where two more siblings were born. The youngest was still in nappies when mum declared, *"I need to have an operation and will be away for a few months. You will have to take care of the babies."*

My grades suffered because of months off school, and I felt resentful.

At thirteen, the most damaging abuse began. Mum boldly announced, *"Hazel needs a bra,"* at the dinner table, drawing attention to my developing womanhood. My desperate pleas for a lock on the bathroom door were ignored, despite being caught naked several times when Dad *"accidentally"* barged in.

Night times were the worst. Often, I hoped my sister would be the target, rather than me, as I struggled to fight off Dad's approaches. *"If you make a noise or tell anyone, I will go to prison, and you don't want that,"* he threatened. Determined not to show emotion, my resolve to leave home intensified. I focused on studying and revising for exams, determined to become a top-level student once more.

At eighteen, I left home armed with eight 'O' Levels, having worked since I was sixteen. By 21, I felt hopeless, losing myself in vodka, cigarettes and unhealthy junk food. Dark thoughts circled my mind: 'what was the purpose of my life? Would I be better off dead?'

Almost throwing myself under a speeding truck was a major turning point. That moment of despair turned into a powerful realisation that something needed to change. A voice in my head shouted, *'Surely there is more to life than this?'* I concluded that if I wanted a better life, I had to make it happen. I ditched a toxic boyfriend, changed my job, and began a fantastic career.

Work-life

Through sheer determination, I rose from a managerial position, secured in my 20s, to becoming a shareholding director in my 40s, smashing a few glass ceilings. Not bad for a girl from a council estate who, at sixteen, was told by her parents, *"Get out to work and bring some money into the house."* Anything is possible if you set your mind to it!

Married life

Like many, I didn't get marriage right the first time. In my mid-20s, I married a handsome man I had met through work. Eventually, we discovered our ambitions differed; he wanted to live abroad, but I didn't. Our twelve-year relationship ended with an amicable divorce. The golden lesson from this part of my life is to be open about what you want and need and always be true to yourself.

Motherhood

Growing up as the eldest of five, I assumed I would become a mother one day. I was well into my 30s when my biological clock kicked in. In an unstable relationship, I decided if it came to it, I would rear a child on my own. Despite my lack of precautions, none came. After ten years, I broke off the relationship, had medical tests and discovered I had multiple fibroids and endometriosis.

Physically, I healed quickly from the hysterectomy, but dark thoughts returned. I was single, in my 40s, childless, and never going to be a mum. Feeling hopeless and isolated, I went for counselling.

"When you think of family life, what comes to mind?" asked the therapist. Pent-up emotions from my childhood flooded out, followed by numbness. Progress was slow.

After months, the therapist asked, *"What are the benefits of not having children?"*

Gradually, it dawned on me that I had time, money, and energy at my disposal. When I managed to reframe my thinking, the solution came: I had to find voluntary work that involved children!

After researching, I found my purpose in becoming a voluntary befriender to children in care and volunteering at sports events run by a charity for children with disabilities. In 2013, I spent two weeks volunteering at three orphanages in Botswana, housing 500 children. The day I left, a letter from a young teenage girl started with, *"Dear Mama..."* My heart swelled, and I felt truly blessed.

The best of times

By my late 40s, my career was going wonderfully well, but my life felt incomplete. I yearned for a loving relationship. Internet dating provided the solution. After finding ways to sort out the honest from the less-than-honest candidates, I struck gold! As Alan walked over to me in the car park in Broadway on 14th June 2006, my heart skipped a beat.

Charmed by his warm Sunderland accent, I found him to be intelligent, confident but not cocky. Slightly taller than me, he had a toned body and similar values. He loved skiing, and so did I. He fancied taking up golf, which I already played. He was divorced with no children – just like me! Could he be for real?

On 21st June, we had our second date – his birthday. Did he have no friends? Months later, I asked, *"Why did you choose to spend your birthday only with me?"* He replied, *"I fell in love with you the moment I saw your dating profile and didn't want to spend my birthday with anyone else."*

Soon, we agreed to become exclusive and began living together in 2008. On the eighth anniversary of our blind date, we got married, making 14th June the most romantic date on our calendar. Life was, at last, perfect. I blossomed, surrounded by the love and affection I had never known before. I felt like a giant. Feeling loved, safe and proud, I was certain I would grow old with this gorgeous man by my side.

The worst of times

The bombshell came on 21st November 2017. With just a weak right arm as a symptom, Alan was told he had six months to two years to live. He had motor neurone disease (MND). He was just 62. Gripped by shock for several days, we cried in each other's arms for hours. Alan kept saying, *"This isn't fair on you."*

Willingly, I spent 18 months doing everything for Alan while his body slowly became 100% paralysed. I nursed him as he became dependent on a ventilator to breathe. I fed him liquid food down a tube in his tummy when he stopped swallowing. I became his advocate when his voice stopped working, and health services and care companies needed lobbying.

"It is what it is, so let's make the best of a bad situation," we said, through everything MND threw at us, determined to live Alan's remaining time to the full. Even when Alan was in a wheelchair, we maintained an active social life. We took

holidays in Vietnam, Scotland, Whitby and Wales. *"Where there's a will, there's a way,"* was our response to the challenges these trips created.

I worried about a future without Alan but learned to manage such thoughts and cope with the fear that he could die suddenly by living in the moment, making the most of every day. It didn't change anything when I cried till my eyes ached or screamed till my throat hurt when no one was around. Alan would die way too soon, and neither I nor the health profession could prevent it.

As unbearable as the thought was, I had to accept that I would live the rest of my life without the man who truly loved me.

"I love you," Alan always told me at the end of every day. When the paramedics took him to hospital with suspected pneumonia in March 2019, my heart ached when he declared, *"If this is it, I want you to know the last thirteen years have been the best years of my life."* A few weeks later, whilst being cared for at a hospice, MND stopped his voice from working.

When I visited Alan on 5th June – a few days before our fifth wedding anniversary – he looked strange. He could not communicate his needs, and I struggled to fathom what he wanted. He looked deeply into my eyes for several minutes. Gently, a nurse said, *"It's time."* I climbed onto his bed and wrapped myself around his frail body. *"I love you with all my heart, Alan,"* I whispered as I kissed his face. He took a breath in, and then nothing. He was gone.

I felt stunned but calm. Dr Kathryn Mannix's book, *"With the End in Mind,"* had prepared me for this moment, but still, it was a shock. I had dreaded this day for eighteen months. I could not feel my breath. Was I still alive?

Celebration of life

Determined his funeral would not be a sad occasion, I invited everyone to wear something bright. Alan's song choices, *"Comfortably Numb"* and *"I've Had the Time of My Life,"* were played at the Church service. People sang along to my chosen song, *"Thank You for the Days."* Sadness overwhelmed me. No sound came out of my mouth as my heart broke into a million jigsaw pieces.

We sang happy birthday as we cut a cake at Alan's wake on June 21st, his 65th birthday and, coincidentally, Global MND Day.

Life after Alan

"How do you feel about me writing a book about your journey with MND?" I'd asked Alan while he was still alive. Deep in grief when Covid came, I set about turning my journal notes into a paperback, knowing I had Alan's blessing. This continuation of my journey, driven by the golden thread of purpose and resilience, helped me find new meaning in life.

Four years after Alan's death, on what would have been his 69th birthday, I self-published *"Life's Good, it's the Disease that's the Problem."* I decided to give all proceeds to the three charities that supported us. The book led to many public speaking engagements, especially after I won an Inspirational Author Award!

Before he died, Alan told me, *"You are to enjoy your life, be spoiled and pampered. You are to find someone you can love and respect, who will love and respect you."* Tough as it was to start dating again in my 60s, good old internet dating found me a man who had been widowed twice. We have become friends.

We understand and respect each other's pain, but neither of us wants to share a home.

Determined not to let the biggest tragedy of my life turn me into a bitter, twisted old woman, I adopt an attitude of gratitude. Through my book and public speaking, I am grateful for the opportunities I have to educate others and advocate for carers, people with MND and the hospice movement.

Even though I wish it could have been for much longer, I have experienced something truly special, something many never have. Alan's love still sustains me; I will be forever grateful for that. Alan's death is my hardest challenge, but it highlighted the golden thread of love that bound us. As much as I miss every aspect of him, he continues to inspire me. Whenever I think of him, I am reminded of the deep joy I felt while he was with me.

Alan's diagnosis and our journey with MND taught me none of us knows what's around the corner. Without being morbid or negative, we should all expect the unexpected and live life to the full while we can. It's incredible how love and courage can forge moments of joy even in the darkest times. When we needed our greatest strength, our love gave it to us.

The choice is yours

The golden thread of my life is woven with resilience, determination and love. These themes have guided me through my challenges and successes and still guide me. They say time is a healer. It is not. I have learned I have to heal myself. I still have bad days – I am a work in progress. But like everyone, I have a choice.

I choose not to be a victim or wallow in self-pity. I choose not to stagnate. I learn from my experiences, find my new tribe, become a new me, and move forward. Each day, I look up, not down. I look forward, not back. I believe it's better for me and everyone around me.

I hope my story inspires you to find and follow your own golden threads, embrace your strength, and learn from your experiences. They will shape your life's journey.

About Hazel

Born in North Devon and now living in Solihull, West Midlands, Hazel is an educator, philanthropic public speaker, author, Trustee of the MND Association, and advocate for carers, hospices, and people living with MND.

"Life's Good, it's the disease that's the problem" is only available from **https://lifesgoodbook.co.uk** with 100% of funds donated to MND Association, Marie Curie and Myton Hospices.

Chapter 8

Delight in Being Fully Present

by Jean Wolfe

We are playing, both on the floor. The train comes out of the station, making chff chff noises. It travels along the track through the cardboard tunnel, then ascends a 45% angle, the noises growing louder. The track has disappeared, but the train continues slowly upward over an atlas, stopping when it reaches the stool at the top. We are both absorbed in what is happening.

Another train swoops down from the air to the stool. They join each other magnetically with a click. We catch each other's eye. From nowhere, we reach the same place. We laugh – me and my nearly three-year-old grandson – and share a special moment without words.

Then, the descent begins.

This scene looks like a muddle on the floor, which should have been tidied up. The train does not stay neatly on the wooden track; it is created from books and, in this case, an atlas. When I say *"playing together"*, you might imagine a defined game with rules like Snap or Snakes and Ladders. But he is a bit too young for that. Anyway, I think this kind of imaginative play is a more rewarding experience. It is better for him and better for me.

When I say we're playing together, I really mean I take turns and fill in with ideas, but my main role is to be the witness and simply to be very, very present. These moments can be fleeting and often get crowded out by the hustle of life, but they are very satisfying.

I am lucky to be able to spend this time with him. I am no longer cooking meals for six people every day, working solidly, or spending hours on the school run, but reflecting back, it is the sort of experience I have valued at every stage of my life.

Why be fully present?

You find huge relief in not worrying about the past or anticipating the future. World events that we see through the screen are frightening, and anxiety seems to be on the rise in every age group. Any respite from distress is a bonus for our mental and physical welfare. The present is a present (gift) to yourself. You are free to engage with what is around you. The cognitive part of your brain can relax, and your subconscious comes to the fore.

When you are present to another person without judgement, they feel validated. Whether talking or silent, they feel they matter. We have all felt the snub when someone looks over our shoulder for someone more important or stares at their phone mid-sentence. Being fully present is often the biggest gift you can give to a person. Your ego is out of the way, and you are not even deciding on your response while they are talking. The importance of being present is a golden thread that has informed my life.

Discovery learning – the teacher's role is simply to be present.

I wondered when I was first aware of this idea about being present. One starting place was when I trained as a teacher and learned about *"discovery learning."* This idea is that what children find out for themselves is more vital and meaningful than learning by rote or being told about principles. I had an orthodox education with little opportunity for much discovery, so these were new and exciting ideas.

I remember my excitement when learning about Wordsworth and discovering who he met and was influenced by. I found the huge reference books in the school library – which I had never noticed before – that led me to another thinker and then to another. Honestly, I can't remember anything factual, but the feeling of making connections without being directed or eclipsed by a teacher who knew it all was a powerful and enjoyable experience.

These days, we might call it kinaesthetic learning or neurodiversity. Still, the concept of *"discovery learning"* included a deep respect for the child and their process, which felt right to me.

Recently, I met a hugely entrepreneurial woman who took over a small art gallery. Her business mentor had asked her to write about her vision for the gallery. She had become paralysed with fear, relived her failures in school exams, and then was anxious about not doing her best for the new venture. We had a conversation, and I listened to her excellent ideas. Immediately afterwards, she was excited to put her ideas into writing. All she needed was someone present without an agenda, and she felt validated and confident.

Being present through improvisation

Jazz musicians are well known for improvising and being so present that they spontaneously create music. In the theatre, rehearsals often start with improvisation around the characters or situation, which helps the actors become fully immersed.

I am part of an improvisation group preparing for a performance. There are no lines to learn; the audience chooses the character and the setting, so the only thing required is to respond spontaneously in the moment. You can't get it wrong. The only worry is that you might not think of anything – but that never happens.

When the audience does not provide prompts, we respond to each other. Audiences can find it difficult to believe it is made up on the spot. One of our *"games"* involves one person on the stage being joined by another who indicates where they are and who they are. The first person accepts what is offered and then builds on it with their own response. A significant component of success is that each person gives their entire presence to others and, in return, receives that from others. This creates a safe group dynamic, and the results are often hilarious. Everyone contributes, which helps everyone flourish.

The impact of early childhood experiences

The life we have in childhood seems normal unless we have an alternative experience. That contrast came from comparing a life where I walked down the village street to school, my family knew everyone, and my mother was a supportive, kind presence. Sadly, she died suddenly, and we then moved to a remote house with no neighbours and no community. I was at boarding school, and my new stepmother seemed to feel that everything I did was wrong.

As a result, I gradually developed alertness to disapproval and vigilance in social situations. I became naturally drawn to support and connect with people with shared values. At the time, it was lucky I was at boarding school, as I had friends, and life was much more straightforward. Also, there was an interesting walk down the village every day, which helped.

Adversity and failure can often contribute more to adult characteristics than success. Although I was very sad about the situation, I believe I developed a sensitivity to others that might not have happened otherwise. My wish to be present for others is partly an honouring of my mother's approach, which I valued more as I felt the contrast of life without it.

I am glad to say that my stepmother and I had a kind of reconciliation. Towards the end of her life, when I went to see her, she was lying in bed with her eyes closed. She couldn't speak, but she responded to my voice and reached out to grip my hand tightly. And she didn't let go. We had barely ever touched before, so it was completely surprising. I assumed she would let go quickly, but she didn't. She held my hand tightly for the whole visit. I took it to mean that all the nonsense for all those years was irrelevant, and she wanted to connect with me. I cried lots of tears all over her bedcovers and was grateful this happened just two days before she died.

Being present to yourself and your best ideas

I mentioned that I enjoyed walking at the beginning and end of the school day. Looking into alleyways and gardens as a break between activities was something I enjoyed even when relatively young. Often, I would arrive back and realise I had some really good ideas. I still enjoy doing this, and I even stop at the end of a car journey to collect any thoughts I have had while driving. I wanted to check if other people felt the same way.

Recently, I posted a short survey on LinkedIn asking where people get their best ideas from. Everyone who answered ran their own business. I felt the obvious places for business people to get inspired would be business books and online. Interestingly, no respondents said this is where they get their best ideas. Some said they get ideas at their desk (6%), and 29% said it was in conversation. However, 65% said they get their best ideas in the shower or walking.

From these results, I assume that when we are not focused on preconceived ideas or reaching a solution but are very present in the activity, our subconscious comes in to help. We tune into different brainwaves and become aware of patterns or connections we have not seen before. Rather than being eclipsed by someone with all the answers, like discovery learning for young children, even as adults, we find it more meaningful to discover our way.

Creating the space to be present to ourselves.

We need the space to be present to ourselves to access our best ideas.

You don't have to sit in a darkened room for hours to give yourself the space. Doing something repetitive that requires little concentration can lead to a breakthrough. I expressed this in the following poem, as it has happened to me many times. Writing it down helped me to notice my own experience with more clarity.

> **Sometimes, I sit at my desk**
>
> Sometimes, I sit at my desk
> Waiting for the words
> Searching for the solution
> That pins it all together.
> I stare out of the window.
>
> Sometimes my fingers
> Write the words
> And my brain follows

Like a faithful dog.
I look on in wonder

Sometimes, I am cutting onions
Chopping mushrooms
Stirring the pot
Thinking of nothing
When I slice through to the idea
And rush for the notebook.
Jean Wolfe©

Notice what you notice

Being present for others is a courteous and thoughtful act. Still, it is also important to extend the same compliment to yourself. Be present to what you are thinking and feeling, and notice what you are noticing in yourself. All of it: good and bad, happy and sad. After all, you are the only lifelong companion you have. Having a friend with you on the journey is much better than a critical foe.

About Jean

Jean Wolfe is the co-author of *"Distinctive Voice—the Fearless Guide to a Wholehearted Blog Worth Noticing,"* a Kindle book on Amazon. She believes women must find their own authentic voice and let it be heard. Jean will soon publish her poems on entrepreneurial life. She has many children and grandchildren and recently moved to Stroud in Gloucestershire. You can find out more about Jean at **https://sparkintomarketing.com**.

Chapter 9

Letting Go and Growing: Appreciating the Hard Parts

by LizaMarie Wilson

Facing an unwelcome milestone

As I entered the building, my heart raced, echoing like a drum in my ears. My mind spun with anxiety. Despite all my soul-searching and preparations, I was still unprepared for this pivotal moment. I was not ready for, and I did not want to face, this unwelcome milestone in my life.

I always knew that one day, we would find ourselves at this exact point, separated by a door. What choice did I have? I could turn back and retreat, freeze, paralysed by fear as the gaping void threatened to engulf me or open the door. Instinctively, I knew opening it would change my life, and I felt completely out of control. Yet, I knew that beyond this door lay the inevitable – a step into an unknown future. Crossing the threshold meant leaving behind the safety of what I had learnt. *'Who would I be without you?'* The thought of facing that unavoidable hole in my life filled me with fear, knowing it would change me forever.

The ache of disconnection

Recently, I had turned 50. For weeks, I called you, only to reach you by voicemail each time. I felt disconnected as I waited to see if you would remember my birthday or fail me again. I longed for you to acknowledge me and celebrate my existence on this monumental day. *"Isn't it a parental duty to call their child on their birthday?"* I fretted. Each year, I acknowledge the birthdays of my own three children. What holds you back from fulfilling this basic parental role? Am I not even worth a phone call to validate and celebrate my existence?

You didn't call. No happy birthday wishes for me. I felt rejected, irrelevant, disappointed and forgotten. A surge of anger stirred inside. Feelings of abandonment and confusion swept over me as I spiralled back to my three-year-old self, weighed down by emotions, struggling to understand. *"Why did you choose to leave me? Did you love me? I promised to be better; why wasn't that enough to make you stay? What made you decide to live behind a different front door than mine?"*

A shift in perspective

"STOP!" I berate myself for being selfish and immature. It's just a birthday. What's wrong with me? Haven't I learned anything? *"STOP!"* I catch myself again, realising this harsh, unforgiving voice belongs to my 49-year-old self. Starting anew, I am open to a different perspective. I begin to think of you instead of focusing on my own hurt. Despite my unruly emotions, I know I genuinely want to connect with you. I love you and yearn to feel your love in return.

Instantly, I feel better, reminding myself that you love me. I know you sometimes forget to call, but I realise you never forget me. I recall when you were in the hospital, enduring pain and choosing to limit connections while you fought for your life. I recognise that our experiences were vastly different. Understanding that you were battling to survive, a burning sense of shame subsumes my earlier selfish feelings. I was wrong to expect a call on my birthday while you struggled to live. I don't deserve to exist, not you.

"*STOP! ENOUGH!*" No more dwelling in the shadows of my past. I am no longer a child, I remind myself, but an adult with responsibilities. I'm tired of being a victim of my past, feeling resentful at what I didn't receive. It's time for change. I want to evolve into a better version of myself who loves and appreciates everything. I want to validate you for all you've done, even from afar and celebrate you for your fight to survive. Perhaps you secretly wish for me to reach out despite your insistence on no contact.

The turning point: choosing love over pain

Reaching 50 marks a turning point for me—moving from who I was to who I want to be. I get to choose how I experience my birthday. This year, I decided to call you because I can. I gift myself validation and self-forgiveness and commit to celebrating my life with generosity and appreciation for you. You are my gift, and you keep giving and teaching me to become a better person, even in your absence.

The final farewell

With a renewed sense of resolve, I open the door to your hospice room, fearing that today will bring our final goodbye. I sense the moment has come for our final farewell. The term *'Circle of Life'* symbolises the interconnectedness of all living things, encompassing the cycles of nature – birth, death and renewal. A geometric circle is a continuous curve, equidistant from the centre, with no beginning or end. My *'Circle of Life'* intersected with yours at my birth when you first introduced yourself as my dad.

In my mind's eye, I see you moving restlessly, no longer concealing your impatience or disinterest in my story of the circle. My heart races, my breaths grow shallow, and I struggle against intense pressure as though the walls of my chest are closing in. I hear your irritated voice: *"Liza, get to the point."* Now, a deep sense of urgency and fear tighten around my throat, making me scared of stumbling over my words and leaving me overwhelmed by the rising dread within.

I hear music playing softly in your room but can't discern the tune. I see people around us, but their faces blur, and I can't remember who they are. I'm physically present, yet time seems to have lost all meaning, and I have no sense of how long I've been here. Time stands still, and I find myself longing for the familiar anxiety of stumbling over my words as you urge me to reach the point. But you are still here, and the words I desperately need to express my feelings remain out of reach.

I lean over you, placing my hand on your heart, feeling a silent communication between us – a final grasp for my attention. I hear you saying, *"Liza, it's time for you to go."* At that moment, I realise I am receiving one of life's greatest lessons. *"Dad, I'm getting straight to the point,"* I whisper, as I finally understand through our spiritual connection how to let go. I see now that you are asking me to release you to allow you to move on to the next part of your journey. Suddenly, it is abundantly clear what I must do, and I recognise how much I have resisted this moment.

Kissing your forehead, I whisper, *"I love you, Dad. I'm okay, and I'm letting you go now."* As I walk around your bed, it feels like I am entrusting you to your devoted wife, just as you once walked me down the aisle to give me away. As I gently close the door behind me, I know it marks the end of your circle and a new beginning in mine, shaped by the love and lessons you leave behind.

Tears trickle down my face, leaving a salty taste on my lips. My eyes are red and puffy, and my life feels irrevocably changed. Exhaustion overwhelms me; my body craves nothing. My chest tightens, my breath feels choked, and I'm engulfed in a tsunami of sorrow. From a depth I can't reach, an infinite void seems to open, threatening to consume me.

I will never see you again. As this realisation sinks in, my hero falls, and the emotional skyscraper that supported my identity collapses, shattering into scattered fragments that fall into the cracks of what was once my foundation. Pain, I realise, can be tended to, much like a garden—weeded, watered, and cared for. But suffering is a choice, often rooted in our resistance to letting go.

I can see clearly now how I've been trapped by my inability to release the pain I experienced at three-years-old when you first left my life. Your final departure has brought true PAIN – a raw, pure emotion distinct from the dirty, sticky, unresolved grief of my childhood. I'm grateful that you lived and died by the beach, a place where I have found healing by simply sitting and observing nature.

Waves of grief

Grief ebbs and flows like the sea – unpredictable and varying in intensity. I never know when a wave will hit, how powerful it will be, or how often it will surge. Sometimes, I am caught off guard, tumbling onto the sandy floor in emotional turmoil, unsure which way is up. Swallowing salt water and gasping for air, I struggle to find my footing, only to discover my knees are grazed, and I am bruised and battered with sand lodged in unexpected places.

Yet, I have learned the importance of finding balance within myself. Now, when the waves come, I trust that I'm grounded and can choose how to respond and adapt to my experience without being overwhelmed. I feel balanced and joyful, leaping over the waves as they come, remembering how we used to do this together. You would hold my hand tightly, lifting me as we soared over the waves, laughing and relishing our summer holidays at the beach. I can also be brave, like when I rode the waves to shore, confident in my ability to withstand their force.

Sometimes, I sit and watch the waves roll in, each different in direction, shape, and size. I observe the ocean's natural ebb and flow, aligning my breath with its rhythmic expansion and contraction. As I taste the salt in the air, a calming presence rises in my chest, wrapping around my wounded heart and holding its broken pieces together.

I watch the waves break, forming white, soap-like foam on the wet sand, then retreat as the water seeks to reconnect with its source. Feeling the sun's warmth on my shoulders, I appreciate the power and beauty of my surroundings. I am aware that you, too, will reconnect with our source, and I embrace the cyclical nature of life—its ever-changing times, seasons, experiences, and emotions.

Setting boundaries and self-love

Setting and communicating boundaries is a healthy form of love and self-care. It creates the necessary space to grieve, complete emotional processes, and adapt to change—elements essential for our growth and evolution. While some may see this as selfish, it is a profound expression of self-love. We are each responsible for our self-care, and with that comes accountability for how we handle the changes that life brings.

Life offers us limitless growth opportunities, but it is up to us to recognise and embrace them.

One of my greatest challenges has been confronting and dealing with feelings of abandonment and rejection, of being cheated out of the life I desired. This struggle led to jealousy and envy of those who seemed to have what I was unfairly denied. My rigid expectations blinded me to the fact that I already possessed much of what I desired, disguised in forms I hadn't recognised.

The real question is: How many opportunities do we miss each day because we fixate on what has caused us pain or disharmony? When we dwell on past events, people, or future possibilities, we often close ourselves off to the gifts and opportunities present in the here and now. I invite you to take a moment to reflect on your own golden threads—the moments of pain, love, and growth that shaped you. What is ready to be released?

Becoming your hero

I choose now to follow in your footsteps. As my own hero, I clear the obstacles on my path, embracing transformation and healing. With confidence in my ability to adapt, I continue to grow and evolve, even in your absence. I accept my grief, seek guidance when needed, and trust in the eternal connection with your spirit that lives on within me.

The gift of life is filled with moments and opportunities to choose how we live those moments available to us right now. Life is not an endless gift; it is finite, and we will all eventually grow older and pass on. Yet, within that time, we have the power to determine how profoundly we will grow and how we will choose to respond and evolve as we continue to shape our story.

The gift of letting go

Moving on from an experience or the past requires a willingness to let go, forgive ourselves and others, and embrace a new perspective. Acknowledging what has happened is essential—not necessarily accepting it, but recognising our feelings about it. This openness allows us to welcome new excitement, positive experiences, opportunities, and growth as we move forward. We gain a sense of empowerment by choosing to let go, accept, or forgive.

An affirmation that has supported me through the process of acceptance is: *"I desire and choose to stand in balance, to embrace and accept my feelings. I honour and respect the way I feel. I give myself permission to relax in my body now, knowing I am safe and loved. I choose to relax and am open to forgiveness and seeing things differently."*

Passing on the wisdom

As I step forward into the future, I carry the golden threads of these lessons. I am deeply grateful to my father for loving me and teaching me that, even in the hardest of times, it is vital to validate and accept all my feelings. Equally important is the lesson of letting go; understanding that when you hold on to anything, it will keep you from moving forward, eventually hindering your progress.

I desire to pass this wisdom forward, weaving it like a golden thread into the tapestry of life. I hope this message will uplift you when you most need it and serve as a guiding light to help you remember how to SHINE.

About LizaMarie

LizaMarie's expertise in health, wealth, and relationships, combined with her holistic approach to coaching and therapy, empowers clients to embody their inner wisdom. She helps them release energetic blockages, heal from past experiences, and reclaim balance, enabling them to adapt more confidently, create intentional change, and experience greater joy.

She honours the space between 'no longer' and 'not yet,' and her transformative work nourishes the mind, body, and soul, facilitating emotional healing, growth, and personal evolution.

Chapter 10

Wisdom Gained from a Wheelchair and a Three-year-old

by Paramjit Oberoi

Has there been a time in your life when you formed an unexpected connection with someone in the most surprising circumstances?

2016, I took my daughter Sheenam to Kerala, South India, for Ayurveda treatment. There is no known cure for Juvenile Huntington's disease (JHD), a hereditary disease with which Sheenam was diagnosed a day after her father's funeral in 2002. She was only nineteen. I researched alternative treatments, determined to do whatever I could to bring some comfort and quality of life for my daughter despite this terminal diagnosis.

At this stage of the illness, Sheenam was unable to walk, talk or eat. She was fed through a PEG through her stomach, though, like most of us, she loved her food! As it was too dangerous for her to eat normally, to give her the pleasure of taste, we would soften some food to a consistency which would prevent her from choking.

After about four weeks in Kerala, Sheenam received treatment, began to eat more, and even started to walk a little. This felt truly miraculous. We moved to a homestay near Cherai Beach for a break close to the sea. The nearby restaurant, 'Seaview,' made sure to poach some fresh fish in milk for Sheenam every evening. Although she could only take a few mouthfuls, I was content knowing she could at least taste some food. As a parent, you might understand how difficult it was for me to eat if Sheenam couldn't savour a taste of something.

During our walks on the beach, we noticed the sign for the 'Chilliout' restaurant, which was aptly named because they left the chilli out of the food. In the past, we had decided not to eat there as the restaurant stairs were unsuitable for a wheelchair. One day, as we approached the restaurant, two young lads outside watering the garden greeted us. We stopped and said hello.

"Are you wanting to come in, Aunty?" said one, an endearing term used by younger people to address older ones in India. I looked at Sheenam; she smiled and nodded. Without hesitation, the two lads shouted up the stairs: *"We need your help; come down."* Two more young lads came down, and within seconds, all four of them picked up Sheenam's wheelchair and swirled her up the stairs. No health and safety checks are needed!

Sheenam was chuffed, not only because our table overlooked the Arabian Sea, but also, more importantly, because four handsome men lifted her. She was in her element, and I was grateful to them. I experienced pure delight seeing Sheenam receive attention from the waiters and enjoy a hamburger prepared to just the right consistency.

As I fed Sheenam the last bite and prepared for her PEG feed, I watched a little boy, who had been looking over at us, walk tentatively towards us. Intrigued, he began to play with her wheelchair. Sheenam smiled and put her arms up to him. He came back to explore, then dashed over to his Mum. This beautiful lady, dressed in a crisp white top, came over with her son.

"Hello, I hope you don't mind my son playing with the wheelchair," she said as Sheenam held out her hand to encourage him to play. "My son has never seen a wheelchair and is intrigued."

"It's absolutely fine; Sheenam loves children," I replied. "What's your boy's name?"

"It's Nanu, and I'm Geraldine." She pointed to a majestic gentleman in a white T-shirt coordinated with a white lungi (sarong) trimmed in gold. He walked over to us.

"This is my husband, Deepan."

"Pleased to meet you. I am Paramjit. This is my daughter Sheenam."

While he went back to sit with his friends, Geraldine and I got to know each other. We turned Sheenam's wheelchair to face the sea so she could watch Nanu play with the pebbles. Nanu connected with Sheenam in his own way by placing coloured pebbles from the beach in her lap. Their beaming smiles reinforced this charming thread of connection.

I felt physically tired from supporting Sheenam's Ayurvedic treatments, pushing the wheelchair on uneven ground, and not getting a good night's sleep. For the last couple of days, I had sent an intention to the universe that I could go to a retreat centre to rejuvenate myself.

Nanu and Sheenam were enjoying a complimentary ice cream given by the restaurant. I basked in the sea breeze, the warm sun smothering my face. As the warmth seeped through my skin, I began to feel human again. Surrounded by the chatter in the restaurant, I realised it was the human connection I was missing. Geraldine and I connected quickly. Our deep conversations about life made it feel as if we had known each other for a lifetime. Confiding that I was tired and looking for a retreat, I asked if she could recommend anywhere.

As Geraldine and Deepan left, they wrote down the address and telephone number for Big Banana Island Retreat and invited us to meet them there at 2:30 p.m. the following day. Big Banana Island Retreat was about an hour away from Cherai Beach.

The next day, we called Saju, the amazing tuk-tuk driver we had come to know during our stay. He arrived in his shiny green and yellow tuk-tuk. Although I could not speak Malalaym, the native language spoken in Kerala, and he didn't understand English, it only took five minutes for us to understand each other. He was patient and supportive; nothing was too much trouble. He would gather a few local men to lift Sheenam into the tuk-tuk and fold her wheelchair at the back of the vehicle.

We made a genuine connection at a human level; his smile and willingness to support us made our lives easier. Despite the bumpy ride, the journey through palm and coconut trees, lush greenery and lakes was joyful. When Saju got lost, the detour he took was just what we needed. We were excited to see fresh coconuts by the roadside. We stopped to buy two, experiencing the pure delight of drinking refreshing coconut water through a straw. Saju was grateful for the unexpected stop and enjoyed the treat. Nevertheless, Saju and I exchanged glances of relief as we approached the sign 'Big Banana Island Retreat' at the end of the winding road.

Geraldine, Deepan, and Nanu greeted us with beaming smiles. They unfolded the wheelchair and helped Sheenam out, accompanying us along a path with lush green trees and vivid red, yellow, and pink flowers. Kerala is known as 'God's own country', and true to its name, nature showed off its true colours. Geraldine ordained Sheenam and me with garlands made of fresh flowers. I felt overwhelmed by the warm welcome.

My heart jumped for joy as we approached the thatch-roofed, open-air restaurant overlooking the Periyar River. It felt like pure paradise, as though this place was designed for us. A strange feeling of déjà vu overtook me. I had seen this place in my dream and now came *"back home."* It was as if the whole river dripped from my eyes. Instantly, I knew this was where I could rest my weary head and find peace and solace. We had found our heaven on earth.

One of the staff served us a delicious sweet dish, beautifully presented on a banana leaf, with some Indian tea. It was an exquisite welcome.

Deepan and Geraldine had not mentioned they owned Big Banana Island Retreat, which attracted me to these genuine, caring, and humble people. Their philosophy of simplicity, honesty, and supporting others truly resonated with me. I believe our meeting was orchestrated by the universe. By chance, they had taken a group of retreatants for lunch at Chilliout on the same day and time that Sheenam and I happened to go there.

Nanu and Sheenam were the conduits for our fantastic connection. One by one, the golden threads of our lives have intertwined to weave a beautiful picture of genuine connection and family friendship. Our bond has strengthened since then, with my wider family. I have returned to Big Banana Island Retreat regularly, and Deepan and his family have stayed with me several times. Nanu now calls me Grandma.

The yoga sessions, energising and soothing Ayurvedic treatments and homemade nutritious food have given me a new lease of life. The retreat is so connected to nature that the fruit tree I planted on one of my visits blooms when I'm well and wilts when I'm not. This has happened a few times. Initially, I thought it was just a coincidence when Deepan told me he knew I was unwell because the tree had informed him. However, this has since happened on many occasions, reinforcing the importance of our symbiotic connection to nature.

We have developed a lifetime bond of learning and sharing. Our lives are interwoven and interconnected. I am eternally grateful for this new tapestry born out of the tired threads of adversity.

At home, we had a plaque that said, *"God gave us our relations; thank God we can choose our friends."* Through the adverse circumstances of Sheenam's JHD, we have made many threads of support and genuine friendships worldwide.

Reflecting on my seventy years on this earth, I realise the importance of these connections. Our lives are interwoven with others, creating a rich tapestry of experiences and relationships. Life's true essence lies in these connections, built on authenticity, honesty and integrity.

We are all truly one in a million. Yes, both you and me. The chances of being conceived through fertilising an egg and sperm are one in a million. Each of us is unique, weaving our own intricate tapestry and leaving our indelible mark on humanity. This mark is strengthened by intertwining new and well-worn threads with a base of authenticity.

It begins by listening to that still small voice within, which connects us with our higher consciousness, our soul, a higher power connecting us to the universal source. Through this, our life automatically flows, bringing the right people to us at the right time to help us undo the tangled knots that keep us stuck. Integrity, trust, and honesty in relationships are crucial. These bring out the essence of life and frame the tapestry of life.

Once we connect with our inner being, our true soul, and our essence, we connect with the Universal Power, and there is no stopping us from living our potential. By connecting our magical threads with others at a heart level, we improve the world, operating from a place of loving kindness and true connection.

Through the rich tapestry of my life, I have learned the following strands of wisdom, and I trust that they will resonate with you:

- Ask the universe for what you need
- Be open about your circumstances
- Take advantage of the opportunity to connect at a warm heart and soul level
- Develop a childlike curiosity
- Connect without any expectations
- Focus on the other person rather than being self-conscious about yourself
- Know that threads can be divine interventions
- Don't block gifts that come your way
- Say yes to opportunities
- Have faith that things are in your favour
- Have an open heart and mind
- Be non-judgmental
- Believe that there will be a positive outcome
- Know that a higher force is holding you
- Having a grateful mindset increases the miracles that appear in your life
- Our hearts, minds and souls are connected
- Live in the NOW, and life flows.

These insights have taught me that we are born with nothing, and we die, leaving a legacy in our impact on our world through our interconnected threads of life.

About Paramjit

As an End-of-Life facilitator and life coach, Paramjit is passionate about supporting people in living their true potential and encouraging them to leave a mark on the world by living a legacy of their true worth. Paramjit strongly believes in a higher universal force and walks in faith, courage, and acceptance in equal measure. Her attitude of gratitude has enabled her to develop strength from the adversities she has faced and inspires hope and courage in others.

Chapter 11

To Diagnose or Not to Diagnose? That is the Question.

by Pollie Rafferty

February 2023, just nine days before my 50th birthday, felt like the culmination of a lifetime. I found myself sitting in a room that seemed to mirror the turmoil within, with peeling magnolia paintwork, cracked brickwork and patches of mould in the corners. A slight chill hung in the air. I had waited three long years for this moment, but it felt like I had been waiting my entire life.

For three hours, I spoke with the woman opposite me and occasionally with the lady on my right, who furiously typed everything that was said. A small pile of neatly folded tissues sat in front of me, but otherwise, the table was free of distractions.

This was one of the hardest conversations I had ever experienced. My leg jiggled up and down nervously. I wanted to get up, to pace the room, but I couldn't. I felt trapped in my chair, tears welling in my eyes as my breath caught in my throat. A thousand thoughts clambered around my mind: *'What if? What then? Why did I do this? Will it make a difference? What if they tell me I'm just being stupid?'*

Reflecting on the past

When my daughter was a tiny baby, she would cry If held too long. She was content to be left to her own devices; she refused to use a dummy and only took a bottle a couple of times. Deep voices, even her beloved Grandad's, would make her cry.

She was our firstborn, so as parents, we didn't really know any different. As she grew, she started to explore the world. While other little ones would stick close to their parents, she would be on the other side of the room, organising her toys alongside other children but not properly playing with them. When I mentioned my concerns, people would say, *"Oh, my kid does that."* So, I would think I was just being oversensitive.

When my daughter started nursery, I thought the staff might notice something, but they only said she was bright, clever, and doing well. Concerned with doing the right thing, she would get very upset if she thought she had done something wrong. This anxiety would sometimes lead her to get angry, lash out, and stop doing things.

When she started primary school, I told the teachers that she wasn't naughty; she just wanted to do the right thing so badly. Over the years, her differences became more obvious, and the teacher eventually recommended a referral. My daughter was diagnosed as autistic in the summer of 2016. This diagnosis marked the beginning of a long journey – not just for her, but for me as well. It was the beginning of a new thread in my life's tapestry that led me back to myself. As I unravelled her story, I found that it deeply intertwined with mine.

Personal realisations

I have always felt different, on the edge, like an outsider looking into other people's worlds, not quite fitting in. I would regularly stand out, and not always for the right reasons! I didn't understand many jokes, especially those made at someone else's expense. The elephant in the fridge joke, for example, always baffled me. How would an elephant get into my house? I was puzzled. It's not native to my country and wouldn't fit through the door, let alone climb into the fridge. And if it did get in, there would be no kitchen or fridge. And, as we have margarine, not butter, would it still leave footprints?

My invisible friend was a pet dog, not another child or person. I spent hours in the garden, catching grasshoppers or sitting quite still, hoping a bird would sit on my finger. I even made a Lego playground for spiders. Obsessed with animals, especially dogs, I learned all I could about different breeds. If I thought I had done something wrong or got told off for being naughty, I would dissolve into puddles of sobbing distress.

In school, I drifted along, doing my best to obey the rules and not stand out because that was what was expected of me. I didn't want to get into trouble or disappoint my parents. I felt like I wasn't normal, but I desperately wanted to fit in. I stared out of windows, inventing stories or daydreaming, running conversations through my head. I was constantly frightened of saying or doing the wrong thing or being perceived as odd.

I joined in, hanging out with other kids and doing what they were doing, even if I couldn't understand why. I agreed with whatever they said so that I would be liked. The thought of not being liked terrified me and still does. I felt different at school, and it became uncomfortably apparent that socialising was not for me. So, I dived into the realms of fantasy. I loved books and disappeared into other worlds at any opportunity, living a life of adventure through their pages. I loved running with elves and dwarves, fighting bad guys and righting wrongs. Dungeons and dragons became almost more real to me than life itself. I could feel more *"me"* when role-playing than just being myself.

Challenges of adulthood

The confusion of my childhood carried on into adulthood. Things didn't get easier; in fact, they probably got harder. Desperate to find somewhere to fit in, I became vulnerable. I was groomed into a relationship at sixteen with a 36-year-old man. This relationship became abusive, coercive, and controlling. After 7 years, I escaped, thinking I was finally free – only to face another silent battle with deepening anxiety and depression. I reached a point where I couldn't leave my house or go into the back garden.

I had burnt out and was diagnosed with social anxiety, depression, a mood disorder and chronic fatigue syndrome. I felt defeated. Yet, each setback and each moment of self-doubt became a thread in the fabric of my resilience. Friendship and storytelling helped me overcome this latest challenge, enabling me to return to work part-time.

Determined to move forward, I eventually found a supportive relationship with a man who accepted me as I am, with all my quirks and misunderstandings. He supported me in all I did, especially storytelling. We moved to the south coast, and at 35, I gave birth to my daughter. By this stage, I had almost given up on my dream of a normal life with a house, a job I loved, a loving partner, a washing machine and kids.

A new understanding

My daughter's diagnosis wasn't a big surprise. I have been researching autism, especially how it manifests in women and girls. However, I was surprised at how it resonated with my own experiences of growing up and all the things I could tick off. I found myself saying repeatedly: *"That's so me! I did that! I feel like that!"* Realising how many of the little traits that shouted at me from the books I had hidden or tried to hide, I couldn't ignore the signs any longer: *"I'm autistic, too."*

I recognised myself more and more. I noticed how I would not understand subtle cues when consciously making eye contact and how my internal dialogue never stops. I became aware of other things like my absolute hatred for a certain fork, where using it makes me feel physically uncomfortable. I recognised my inability to cope with busy public transport or crowded rooms unless I was talking or telling a story on stage. Each memory, each realisation, was like pulling a thread from the tapestry of my life. With each pull, my image of myself changed, revealing the patterns I had never understood.

I started opening up to others, expressing what I was thinking. Their reactions varied: *"You don't look autistic," "You're not autistic"," What makes you think you're autistic?"* Though I tried to explain, it was hard to describe how I felt as I was learning about it myself. The reactions I received were similar to when I had expressed concern about my daughter. I would often be told. *"I don't like crowds or public transport,"* or *"I don't like XYZ, and I'm not autistic."*

The hardest conversation was with my Mom. It stopped me from seeking a diagnosis for a while. When I mentioned my concerns to her, her response was a flat *"NO."* I didn't want to upset her or make her feel like she had let me down as a child. The information wasn't there when I grew up. Autism was thought to be a boys-only condition, like in the film Rain Man.

Finding freedom

As women, we're often expected to blend in, to smooth out the edges that make us different. For years, I thought my struggles were just a part of being *"bad at normal,"* but perhaps it was the world that didn't know how to see me. As I waited for the woman opposite to speak, some of these thoughts flashed through my mind. What If she agreed with other people and the things I had told myself? *"Why am I doing this now I'm older?"* I asked myself.

When she finally opened her mouth to speak, the words I had been both hoping for and dreading came out: *"You are autistic. All the information you have provided, the forms you've completed and our conversation today confirm it. Oh, and have you been tested for ADHD? If not, we would suggest you do."*

I released a breath I didn't realise I had been holding as tears flowed down my cheeks. I wasn't broken! There was a reason I had struggled all my life. I wasn't lazy! My brain was wired differently, making it more difficult to do certain things. I felt a huge weight I had carried all my life had been lifted. Now, I could start looking at myself with kindness instead of hate and compassion instead of criticism. At last, I had understanding!

I had spent years behind a mask of *"normalcy"* that hid my true self. Since the diagnosis, I have allowed myself to unmask a bit at a time. I'm learning to be more authentically me, to stop repressing my actions quite so much, allowing myself time to recover and pace myself. Getting that diagnosis has been the best thing I have ever done.

Encouragement to others

For so many reasons, I almost didn't go through with the diagnosis. Although I felt deep down that I was autistic, I felt unable to claim it without the diagnosis. But I did it for me, for my daughter, and now, by sharing my story with other women who are unsure about seeking a diagnosis.

If you are concerned, I recommend not listening to those who say that you don't look or act autistic. They don't know you. You have spent years masking, trying to fit in and be *"normal."* You may not even know yourself in the way that you need to. Listen to that voice if you have an underlying feeling of unease, a sense of not fitting in, or find it hard to understand the world around you.

Don't listen to the people who say you have lived your life without a diagnosis, so why do you need one now? For me, it has been freeing, eye-opening and life-changing. I feel more myself at 50+ than I ever have. I have stopped worrying so much about what I should be doing and focused more on what I want to do – the things that make me happy, without guilt or wondering if it's *"normal."* I no longer try so hard to fit in. I share my story and diagnosis when I need to and explain how it might affect our conversation.

I give myself permission to be myself. If you can do that without a diagnosis, great! If you can't, take the steps needed to become the person you are meant to be. Like me, get a formal diagnosis and find the support you need to rediscover yourself in a kinder, gentler and more understanding way.

About Pollie

Known globally as the Speaker's Storyteller, Pollie is an international speaker, storyteller and creator of the STAR Storytelling system. She is a youth worker with a diploma in narrative therapy and a qualification in psychology. Her passion is the power of storytelling and how it can be harnessed to empower young people to create a better future. She is also passionate about raising awareness so that what happened to her as a young person doesn't happen to others.

Chapter 12

My Wonderful Life. My Wonderful Future

by Rachel Hardy

Life is unpredictable. It has a way of shaping us into who we are meant to be. It's taken me until my mid-50s to reflect on and understand what I want from life. I realise that the different strands of my life: work, two marriages and divorces, friendships, family and hobbies have helped me to understand what truly matters.

I have known a group of friends since my late teens, and I remember our earlier idealistic view of life. It's fascinating to see how we have evolved in ways we could not have imagined in our carefree nightclubbing days. Perhaps you can relate to our biggest worries back then – what to wear and how to get to work with a hangover the next day?!

Like most people, I have experienced both good and bad.

Being blessed with a wonderful family is one of the best things. I won the lottery of life—my parents, brothers, grandparents, cousins, aunts, and uncles are all constants in my life. I am fortunate to have most of them still here with me. I've built another family of people who are not related and who are also constants in my life. We don't necessarily see each other often, but we understand each other.

Though unplanned, my career in NHS finance was very successful and fulfilling. Being an accountant was the last thing

I aspired to do. I hated maths, but my fascination with the NHS and the many wonderful people I met sustained my career. My work was mentally sustaining and well-paid. It happened organically, underpinned by hard work. I loved the mental stimulation of work and the cut and thrust of working with different people. I relished a challenge, and I got many. I was persuaded to take on senior roles I would never have considered. They involved delivering extremely difficult projects and working alongside many people. I realised I was skilled at delivering complex projects and relished working with people from different backgrounds. It was an interesting time which showed me my true potential.

I have always been very fit and healthy. I enjoy the tranquillity of yoga alongside the competition of outdoor sports such as golf and tennis, relishing the feeling of the elements on my skin.

I have a beautiful home that I created from a blank canvas. I have chosen colours that have a sumptuous and cosy feel and have created a feeling of comfort and security that I have not always felt. Owning and building a home on my own was a liberating and healing experience in the difficult aftermath of divorce. I found and realised my strength, resilience, and freedom as an individual, an experience that would have floored many people.

I have had money, freedom, and choice (even if I haven't always realised that), plentiful food, extensive travel, and many opportunities, which I have fully embraced.

I have experienced an abundance of love during my life, sometimes enduring, sometimes fleeting, but it was still love. I love deeply and fiercely.

The challenges that I have faced have taught me valuable lessons about myself.

I have had two marriages, both of which ended in divorce. I never thought I would ever get divorced. I believed that marriage was a lifelong commitment. My family and friends set this template for me. However, life had different plans, teaching me that sometimes the bravest thing you can do is to walk away.

The shame of one divorce, let alone two, affected me profoundly in a world where women were judged for their success through marriage, having children and building a family. I felt ashamed and felt like a failure.

One marriage was complicated and abusive over a sustained period. I've dealt with infidelity numerous times (his), coercive and manipulative behaviour (also his), miscarriage, infertility, several rounds of IVF, adoption and unwanted childlessness. I believe the saying 'a murderer will kill you, a thief will steal from you, but you never know where you stand with a liar' is true. I found it so undermining to my self-esteem and sense of self. At times, I felt like my soul was being sucked out of me.

Yet something inside me refused to be beaten, no matter how hopeless things felt. I survived and am here to tell the tale, stronger and wiser. The deep hurt and searing pain of not having a child still upsets me at times. I feel sadness and loss bubbling to the surface as I write this. Yet, I have built an alternative, fulfilling life and am determined to make the most of things.

Imagine my relief when I read Jennifer Anniston's account of her journey of trying for a child, which played out in the spotlight's glare. Her description of sadness, desolation and being judged as a failure completely resonated with me. The view of many people that my successful career came at the expense of having children and criticism of me that focused on my childlessness was extremely painful. Until then, I thought it was just me who felt a sense of anguish and anger each time people asked me: *"Have you got children?" "When are you having children?"* or *"Are you trying for children?"*

Whenever a colleague asked these questions, I would try to respond in a jokey way while feeling a knife turning inside me.

I can't describe my feelings at 44 years old when my ex-husband pulled out for a second time from a final offer of an adopted baby. Everything felt flat and numb following the final conversation, informing the social worker that my husband could not proceed with the adoption. Sitting at my desk in an open plan office amongst colleagues working their usual day, I accepted that I would never have children. I decided to draw a line under this part of my life there and then. *"I am going to get on with my life, whatever that looks like,"* I resolved, despite the bleakness and despair.

You can imagine the mixed feelings of jealousy and sadness mingled with joy and excitement when I welcomed the children of friends and family into the world. Rather than choose bitterness, I decided to be happy and embrace them. I have never regretted that decision. I have lovely young people in my life. I can honestly say, *"I desperately wanted children, but it didn't happen for me."*

As Jennifer Anniston put it, *"That ship has sailed."* I no longer dwell on it.

Perhaps you can relate to this, especially when I say it was a major turning point in my life. After 15 years of uncertainty and heartache, desperately trying acupuncture, health diets, and yoga – I was finished with it. A strange mixture of sadness and relief swept over me. *"You have given it your best shot; you couldn't have done any more,"* I told myself.

Little did I realise I was also drawing a line under my marriage. It may have taken a couple of years to leave, but leave I did. This marked the start of a much happier life.

I don't dwell on the past now; I focus firmly on the next stage of my life and what I have learned. I feel stronger and happier than ever, and I know that life will keep getting better.

How have my experiences changed me?

I know that life isn't meant to be difficult and complicated. It's meant to be joyful, and individuals are meant to be free, even in a relationship and in a family.

I don't feel the need to fit in anymore. I feel confident and happy with who I am. Although it feels good to be liked, it's no longer a defining thing for me. *"Am I happy with myself?"* is my key question. I recognise when I am not being true to myself, such as gossiping, getting irritable with people, or not taking opportunities that come my way. In those situations, I tune into my feelings and reflect on what I could have done differently.

I have learned much from reading and listening to podcasts. Messages that have interested me include: 'Be authentic,' and 'Know your boundaries.' Intellectually, I understood this, but for a long time, I couldn't embody them. Now, it seems simple: I have decided that I like myself and am honest about my own likes and dislikes. I listen to how I feel inside instead of burying feelings. It is sometimes uncomfortable, but I act on my feelings. The relief from doing so is unbelievable.

Have you ever felt different to many people you meet? I know I have. You can imagine how difficult it was for me at school. I was studious, and my parents were teachers, a major crime that meant I was bullied and called a boffin. I felt different as a female in a very male environment at work, not taking the same approach to work, not being a beer drinker or into football. I still feel different in many social circles as I don't have a traditional family (marriage and children). I felt this acutely for years, but I have come to terms with and accept it now.

Previously, I dumbed myself down to fit in and even felt ashamed and embarrassed about myself and my experiences. Now, I realise I am powerful and intelligent. Even now, I feel the old fears surfacing as I wonder whether to share this writing with others in case of criticism. Old habits die hard! Yet, I know I have dealt with much worse and survived. Let them laugh if they want to.

I no longer fear rejection or compromise. The searing pain I used to feel caused me to stay in unhealthy relationships and friendships for too long. If people belittle me or underestimate me (a recurring theme in my life), I now go inward, tune into how I feel, and choose my way. People may not understand my choices, but that's not my problem. Putting this into practice isn't necessarily easy, but I accept it and move on.

I am a stronger person than I realised even ten years ago. I've come to recognise that I used to completely underestimate myself. I achieve whatever I want but in my own way. I can also accept help and listen to others' points of view more.

Honesty is crucial to me. You never know where you are with a liar, and I will not tolerate it anymore. Always be honest, even if it's ugly. At least people know where they are and can make choices with the full facts.

I no longer need to strive like I have for years. I am financially sound, have a beautiful home, and am brimming with health. I need to wake up and smell the roses. The world is my oyster.

So, when the world is your oyster, what do you do?

I realise that for me, it is surprisingly simple things:

I enjoy what I have: my home, my garden, the countryside around me, lovely food, my health, my family, my dog, and having time to spend with people who matter.

Keep learning new things, not necessarily those I have studied for the last thirty years. I have more brain space and time for the things that interest me now, such as art, history, and getting to know my country.

We live in a big world. Although I have travelled extensively, I still have many places to visit. I will see them through different eyes now. I no longer go on holiday to rest; I explore, open my mind, and experience different things.

I need to use my brain and skills in a completely different way. Although my work has been enjoyable and sustained me over the last 38 years, I need change. I wish to use my skills more creatively and revisit my younger passions, such as writing, talking to and helping people, cooking, food, sports, and animals. I don't know how that manifests in work yet, but I know it will happen.

I recognise that good connections and wonderful social circles sustain me. I love interacting with people; it lifts me up when feeling low. Laughing with my friends and family is one of the greatest things in life—and it costs nothing! I create a wonderful, warm, loving, social family without rushing.

Being in nature. Nothing makes me feel better than being outdoors in any weather, whether walking my beloved dog (a human in a dog suit), enjoying the wonderful camaraderie of playing golf, sitting in the garden, visiting beautiful places, or simply gazing at the water.

Staying healthy and fit. My ongoing love of health and fitness sustains me. Having a strong, fit, healthy body and eating beautiful, nourishing food (with a nice glass of wine and the odd cake thrown in) makes me feel strong and positive. It means I can do all the many things I do in life.

I want to one day build my own home with my partner in a beautiful location designed by us as our haven of peace and tranquillity.

I have a new chapter ahead. It will be different from the last thirty years and be amazing!

As I look to the future with hope and excitement, I invite you to reflect on your journey. Embrace your experiences and find the wisdom in your story.

About Rachel

Hi, my name is Rachel, and I am thrilled to participate in Golden Threads. I have spent many years in a business career, neglecting many creative pastimes I loved as a child. Creative writing was one of my favourite pastimes, and this opportunity has helped me share my experiences and kick-start my writing interest again. I hope you enjoy this as much as I have enjoyed writing it.

Chapter 13

Golden Threads of Serendipity

by Sue Williams

The Unwanted Question

"Who do you consider to be your biggest role model?"

My heart sank at this seemingly straightforward question. It was a staple of workplace training sessions, yet I struggled with it. For some reason, I didn't relate to people in that way. *"People are just people, aren't they?"* I thought. Blushing with embarrassment, I desperately searched my mind for an answer, not wanting to feel foolish in front of my team.

Years later, after taking early retirement, I found myself at a coaching workshop. Reading out a list of my desires in response to a prompt, I did an inner double-take as I heard myself say: *"To be a role model."* 'How did that sneak in there?' I wondered.

A Twist of Fate

Life has a way of leading us where we need to be, sometimes by unexpected detours. I eagerly anticipated a tarot card reading course in the West Midlands. Imagine how my spirits sank when it was abruptly cancelled due to the tutor's illness. Deflated, I aimlessly scrolled online, seeking to fill the now-empty weekend.

Serendipity led me to the website of inspirational teacher Debbie Ford. A few years ago, her teachings on the positives of experiencing negative emotions dramatically changed my perspective. A link to her trained associate coaches caught my eye as I scanned her site. *'I wonder if there are any near me,'* I mused, clicking through. There was a coaching workshop in Bath that very weekend. A surge of excitement rushed through me. This was meant to be!

Nervously, I phoned to enquire, and there was one space left! That was a sure sign. The sun shone brightly as I drove to the picturesque city of Bath, my nerves mingling with anticipation. The honey-coloured stone buildings of historic Bath welcomed me despite anxious moments navigating an unexpectedly tricky hill.

A New Path

This series of serendipitous events led me to that pivotal moment, perched on a squishy sofa, reading my journal aloud to a small group of women. Nodding their heads encouragingly, they didn't find my desire to be a role model odd at all.

Though my recall of that day has faded, the moment's clarity remains. It was the first stitch in a golden thread that would weave through my life in the years to come. Years in which I became a course junkie, spending the money inherited from my parents, who had died about a year apart, on personal development. As someone who habitually stuffed down my emotions, I was like a seeker pursuing a magic pill.

Once again scrolling the trusty internet, seeking local networking groups, I stumbled upon a video promoting *"Damsels in Success."* Intrigued, I attended their next meeting and joined a welcoming group of entrepreneurial women. Through these connections, I sampled an array of different modalities, including archetype work, astrology, and the Emotional Freedom Technique. Gradually, my self-awareness grew, though I was still the quiet one lost in the crowd.

A Call to Action

"I am not spending any more money on courses!" I declared while chatting with another damsel before that month's speaker began. The speaker's passion shone through as she described the ups and downs of her journey to find the diamond within. Despite the difference in our life stories, I experienced an undeniable sense of connection. *"I am not signing up for any more courses,"* I told myself as the other ladies left the room to celebrate Bonfire Night.

Inwardly struggling to quell my urge to enrol, I realised Natasha and I were alone. Despite my resolve, I approached her. *"I feel like I need to sign up for your programme,"* I said, *"but I don't want to spend any more money on courses."* *"I can feel goosebumps all over my arms,"* she replied, *"Sign here."* She was firm and direct, handing me a pen. I complied. This was another stitch in my new tapestry, orchestrated by the universe.

Weaving the Tapestry

While working with Natasha, she held an inspirational event featuring several speakers: *"Believe in Your Dreams, Your Legacy, Your Power."* The germ of an idea sparked within me. *"What do you think about producing a collaborative book?"* I asked Natasha. *"It could feature the stories of the speakers at your event?"* *"Yes, let's do it,"* she agreed enthusiastically.

As I prepared to meet her to discuss this exciting new project, my fingers suddenly moved on the laptop keys, typing a poem, *"Believe!"* Imagine my amazement at typing the words: *"Sue, stand up! Stand up! Be bold be strong. Your talent on a world stage truly does belong."* Once again, it felt like a message from the universe.

The original book idea did not go ahead for various reasons. Still, a message from Natasha about one of the speakers who had already written his story reignited my interest. *'I am meant to write this book'*, the thought flashed through my mind as I reread the discarded *"Believe"* Poem. *'Natasha will write her story, I will write mine, and we also have Floyd's.'* I followed the flow and adopted a mantra: *"Whoever is meant to be in the book will be in the book."*

Initially, the book evolved easily, but then, I hit a wall. Stuck and unsure of what to do next, a friend came to the rescue, printing off the collection of draft chapters. *"This is your book,"* she declared, waving the wad of pages before me. Her encouragement helped me persevere.

A Golden Moment

Fast forward six years to the launch of *"Believe You Can Live a Life You Love at 50+,"* the third anthology in the Believe series. Standing at the side of the room in that same friend's house, I watched, entranced, as each woman approached the box of books and received their copy. The stillness in the room was palpable. Silently, they leafed through the pages, searching for their chapter. Each read their words, tangible in book form, the quiet power of women recognising and owning their personal journeys.

Why have I singled out the third book launch? Because it almost didn't happen…

Faith and Perseverance

It was my 60th year. Excitedly, I planned to launch the book on my birthday, 9th May. It seemed the perfect way to celebrate, holding an uplifting gathering of inspirational women over 50. All role models in their own unique way. I had great plans for the event, as it was to be held in a historic building in the centre of Coventry that one of the authors was trying to save from disuse. There would be powerful but fun touches, including feedback theatre, where performers would reflect the authors' words in movement. Everything was coming together nicely. But life had other plans.

In the build-up to the launch, I commissioned pebbles adorned with uplifting words and phrases to reflect self-belief. On collecting these from the artist, one fell out of the box. *"Oops"*— I just caught it. *"We nearly lost Faith"*, I said jokily, reading the painted word on the stone. Hearing this, the creator's hand flew to her necklace. *"I need more faith. I haven't been to church recently,"* she said, looking sad.

Shortly afterwards, a friend and I visited the planned launch venue to discuss catering arrangements. Something caught my eye on the way into the building. *"That plaque looks a bit like an angel." "Yes, it does"* my friend replied. Chatting to the venue's catering manager, she recounted a story of when she had been down on her luck. As she spoke about darker times in her life, she raised her hand instinctively to her neck. Clasping her necklace, hidden under her blouse, she opened her hand to reveal the words *"Believe"* engraved on a gold disc. *"My friend gave me this. I call her my angel,"* she said. Something lurched inside me. I raised my eyebrows at my friend, whose eyes opened wide, exchanging knowing glances at this mysterious thread of connection.

Storm Clouds Gather

We chatted and explored the venue, visualising where the speakers would stand. As I read a notice, my friend suddenly said, *"Sue, Sue, stand still. I want to catch the sunlight streaming onto you through the window."* I held my position as she snapped her shot, thinking no more of it. The bright sunlight reflected the positive glow sweeping through me at the feeling of everything coming together nicely. Images of the women sharing their stories in this space floated in my mind's eye. However, the distant rumble of storm clouds was gathering.

Busily, I worked on two books, planned the launch, and supported participants in navigating an online 30-day challenge in which I also took part. I wanted to help people to the best of my ability, but an urgent pressure to respond to peoples' comments in the challenge pulled at me. Self-imposed pressure, most certainly, but urgent nevertheless.

Tensions and misunderstandings with a couple of people mounted. Trying to make my feelings clear, I felt a sharp slap of frustration when saying, *"I want either A or B,"* I received a response directly contradicting this with *"I am only prepared to go with C." "What else can I do?"* I worried, the people-please in me wanting to maintain the peace. Increasingly stressed, odd behaviours burst out of the mounting tension.

Breaking Point

Waking anxious and shaking, feeling as if I was having a heart attack one morning, I rang 999. They couldn't hear me properly, and I dropped the phone. A whirlwind of weird situations developed over the coming days, ending with me lying on a trolley in an accident and emergency for hours, describing everything around me. I was a journalist, you see! It was my duty to report on everything. Or that is what I told the medical team a few days later, just before I was sectioned for observation at a mental facility. As I landed there, I gazed at colourful drawings and sketches all around, adorned with words such as Confidence and Belief blazing at me. *"Wow,"* I thought, in awe. *"It's like the Believe books brought to life!"*

The launch was cancelled, and I was devastated. *"It was what I wanted to do to celebrate my 60th birthday",* I sobbed to a friend. One day, I stared in shock at the front page of the daily newspaper. Emblazoned across the front page was a picture of the charred cross at Notre Dame, with a shaft of sunlight shining through the window to illuminate it. Echoes of my friend's photo of me at the venue, which had subsequently closed! Everything seemed to be falling apart. Yet, underneath the picture was an uplifting article stating that more people aged over 50 than ever were entering employment. A curious juxtaposition, I reflected, given the subject of my book. Seeds of hope that something good could rise from the ashes?

Something kept tugging at me over the coming weeks. I knew one of the contributing authors had cancer. An inner voice kept saying: *"You have to do it for her, Sue; you have to finish the book."* These words drove me to revitalise the book, and five months later, we held a beautiful launch at my friend's home.

The woman with cancer was able to attend. She took a deep breath at a sharing session, drawing in the courage to read her story aloud. Hesitantly at first, her voice gained volume and strength with each word she spoke. I felt tears welling in my eyes at her vulnerability in sharing. A wonderful day was spent passing around Believe pebbles, sharing our hopes and dreams and enjoying companionship in the sun. My original devastation at not celebrating the book on my 60th dissolved. This was meant to be.

A Legacy

Within two weeks of the event, the author with cancer died. Reeling from this news, I understood why it had felt so important to keep going. Her story formed part of a wonderful legacy for her family and fellow authors who witnessed her belief and courage. Not only had she been a role model for me, but I also believe I was one for her.

The journey had come full circle, from not being able to name a role model to recognising that we all have the potential to be role models in given circumstances. Serendipity had woven a beautiful tapestry of belief, connection, and perseverance.

About Sue

An ex-civil servant, Sue Williams worked in career education and guidance. She is now a Director of the Book Boost membership for non-fiction authors. She has published three anthology books on self-belief for women and is an Amazon best-selling author for her anthology *Believe You Can Live a Life You Love at 50+* and her award-winning poetry book *I Am Unique*. Sue created the inspirational Believe Oracle Cards and a series of poetry cards.

Chapter 14

Reclaiming the Divine Feminine: My Healing Journey from Endometriosis

by Wenke Langhof-Gold

I am a woman

I had not fully embraced the fact that I was female until the age of eleven. Playing football with the boys and roaming free in the forest made me feel human rather than *a woman*. The reality of my gender hit home when, one day, in utter shock, I found blood on my toilet paper. *"Now you've got that shit, too,"* were my mum's words, welcoming me to the tribe of moon-bleeding humans. Being a woman, I had drawn the shorter straw. Or so it seemed.

A child of the East

I turned from an androgynous child into a female body that bled monthly in socialist East Germany. In the collective ideology of my country of birth, all humans, regardless of their gender, were supposedly equal. Housewives were almost non-existent. Women worked just as hard as men and could do whatever men did. However, the reality looked slightly different, and the women in my family still did all the household chores on top of their normal work hours. Somehow, the equality system had bypassed our men's ability to wash the dishes or do the laundry. Nonetheless, women were, at least on paper, seen as no different to men, which was my belief until November 1989. Just one month after officially becoming a teenager, my world was replaced almost overnight with a completely new one.

Unification – or how to swap one belief system for another

The unification of Germany shattered my known reality. Within six whirlwind months, my socialist framework of reference was replaced by the 'enemy' ideology of capitalism. After our failed experiment of equality amongst humans, we time-travelled back to a society where women stayed home with their children and relied on their husband's income. The weaker sex? Standing behind the man? Chained to the kitchen? So many collective ideas of what a woman should be I did not identify with at all. I was at total odds with this new country I suddenly lived in.

Have you ever felt disconnected from who you truly are? I was bleeding the pain of being a woman in a man's world into sanitary pads as white as my ashen face every moon cycle. The more I tried to fit in, the more I got lost. My once clear blood became dark, smelly, dirty, and full of the pain of all disempowered women. My abdomen felt the pain of all the generations of women who had come before me, who had fought for their right to be equal.

A lineage of strong women

The image of women as somehow inferior to men made no sense to my teenage self. Throughout my life, I had been surrounded by strong women. My Grandmothers had raised children and rebuilt their lives in post-war Germany. As refugees from the Sudentenland, the border region between Germany and today's Czech Republic, they faced immense upheaval. Their men, at war, had been unavailable to be relied upon. These women were warriors, the softest of hearts encased in courage of steel. They had survived as women, supported each other as women, and raised their children among women.

My Mum and my aunties were their daughters. Each of them was much stronger than any man I had ever encountered. I was born into a circle of women. Mothers handing the baton of life over to daughters, passing on the flame of the divine feminine in the perpetual, eternal dance of procreation. It was a celebration of female empowerment. The women around me did not need men to survive. How could I carry this flame into the 21st century?

Losing my power to endometriosis

When I became a mother myself at the age of thirty, my usually painful periods turned into unbearable torture chambers. I was too busy looking after the child my body had produced to notice my own physical and mental decline. The fertile soil of my womb was turning into a desert and losing its ability to create and sustain life.

Initially, I was in self-denial: *"I'm fine,"* I told myself, plodding on with my daily chores. The women in my family had sacrificed their own needs for the well-being of their children. Hardships were to be endured so the next generation could live.

By the time I admitted to myself that I had a problem, endometriosis had progressed to the worst stage medicine can diagnose. According to the doctors, there was nothing they could do apart from removing my womb completely. A hysterectomy at 34. I was not ready for early menopause. I was not ready for hormone replacement therapy. I was not ready to allow the flame of womanhood to be extinguished within me.

Listening to the voice within

Luckily, through the thundering waves of pain crashing over my body each moon cycle, the wise woman we all carry deep within softly whispered into my heart: *'There is another way.'*

I had no idea what this other way was, but I knew I had to listen to this inner voice. Years of searching for the path of healing became years of searching for myself. I had lost myself in the expectations others had of me or in my own illusions of what those expectations were.

Healing from illness was like retracing my steps: back through all the twists and turns of my life. Times where I had taken the wrong path, where I hadn't followed my heart, where I had trusted the judgment of others more than my own. I did not study art because my parents said I would not find a job. Chasing a 'reputable career' when money and material wealth had never been important to me.

It was hard to face all those wrong decisions, the mistakes I had made to end up where I was: crippled in pain, no longer wanting to be on this earth if living meant so much suffering. In the darkness of that suffering, however, I found my light. I realised that there were no mistakes. The wrong turns were exactly the ones I needed to take to learn the lessons my soul came here to learn.

The path to healing

Healing happened when I allowed the beliefs and certainties that had once been the pillars of my world to crumble and fall. What if my parents had been wrong? What if I allowed myself to be creative? What if I let go of telling myself, 'I can't'? What if I started to believe I could?

I started to get better when I allowed the truths I held dear to shift, change, and vanish into the void where nothing existed anymore. Only nothing holds the possibility for everything. From the void, I rebuilt: first my health, then my life. And I saw that the truth I had been searching for had always been there, right in my heart. I just had to trust it and follow its guidance without fear.

I healed. It was a miracle (the doctors claimed), impossible (they said), the exception to the rule (or a living example that maybe the rules were wrong?).

A child of Mother Earth

I didn't feel like a miracle. It wasn't as if health had just dropped out of the sky one day. What healed me were very distinct steps and good old common sense. What healed me was returning to my Grandmother's way of living.

In my childhood, we grew most of everything we ate in our garden. We foraged. We hunted. Life was simple: everything came from Mother Earth directly onto our plate. There was no supermarket middleman. There were no colourful plastic advertising messages filled with preservatives. I had lost my soul and my health in the luxury of Western choice, in the opulence and abundance of superstore availability. It was time to reclaim my truth by remembering my ancestors' wisdom.

I banned anything artificial from my life. Nothing out of a science laboratory was allowed in my body or my home anymore: goodbye processed food, goodbye polyester and acrylic, goodbye household bleach and chemicals.

Everything had to be natural, real, and authentic, including my emotions and beliefs. There could be no more pretence; there could be only pure and honest me. Healing meant being unapologetically my true self.

What did I learn along the way?

Listen to the body. Pain is an instrument with which the universe guides us toward what needs attention. Don't ignore it; listen to what it is telling you. Nobody knows my body as well as I do.

Embrace authenticity. Living true to myself means aligning my lifestyle with my values. It means not giving others the power to tell me what's right for me. If I dare to stand up for my truth, life becomes a fun game for me to play.

Love is the greatest healer. Love and gratitude are the highest frequencies of human emotions. In their frequency range, solutions to all our problems are carried to us, like driftwood being washed overnight onto a beach. These two little questions help me shift into the energy state where all solutions reside:

- What am I grateful for right now?
- Who or what in my life do I love?

Everything is energy. All physical expression is just a temporary manifestation of an energetic frequency. Energy particles exist in all possibilities outside of time and space. My human consciousness forms my beliefs, and my beliefs create my reality. What happens to me is one thing: what I make it mean, and the story I tell myself will shape my reality. I am the author of my story and the director of the movie of my life. I have total control over what I believe and the meaning I attach to events.

Problems are simply growth opportunities. The minute I started viewing problems as opportunities for growth, they ceased to exist as problems. If I asked you to choose between a positive, solution-focused outlook on life and a negative, problem-ridden outlook on life, which one would you choose? What if you genuinely have that choice?

I am what I eat. I eat local, seasonal, organic food and try to eat the colours of a rainbow. I live a life rich in connection and mutual respect for all living things, and I consume with gratitude, honouring the plants and animals that gave their lives to nourish mine.

Move it, baby! My human body is designed to move. Riddled with stage 4 endometriosis, I spent days on the sofa or in bed, a hot water bottle glued to my lower abdomen like a second skin. Waves of pain were washing up on the shore of my being as constant as the ocean tides. The less I moved, the more I hurt. The more I hurt, the less I wanted to move.

I learned that my physical body is designed to move. When I move and exercise, even if it's just a gentle walk, my energy flows freely, keeping the system clean and healthy. Walk, swim, cycle, stretch, dance, play, climb, skip, hop – whatever you do, move.

Water is life. 72% of the human body is made of water. Just as the water in a flowing stream is cleaner than that of a stagnant pond, my body is cleaner and healthier if everything flows. My joints get lubricated with an internal healing fluid; my lymphatic system and blood flow supply nutrients to my trillions of cells and remove toxins from the body, but they rely on water. Drink and be healthy.

Choose joy. Embrace life fully, and seek joy in each moment. At some point in my journey, I consciously chose life over suicide. I decided that if I was to stay on this earth, I would no longer be satisfied with a safe, unfulfilled, limited existence. I wanted to be life in all its powerful and colourful expression. I promised myself joyful, loud, creative living rather than mere survival.

Love yourself. In self-love, the divine feminine reclaimed her power, and finally, I was happy to be a woman. Today, I stand empowered in the wisdom of all women who came before me, embracing my monthly periods with love, self-care and gratitude, remembering some wise words I once read:

"When you realise how perfect everything is, you will tilt your head back and laugh at the sky."

About Wenke

Wenke mentors people from illness to health. In her health and life coaching practice, she helps clients reconnect with the essence of the divine feminine using various energy medicine techniques. Her special areas of interest are endometriosis and cancer. She loves nothing more than gathering like-minded humans around a fire, singing songs and drumming life's heartbeat into circles of human connection. As a child of Mother Earth, she is at home in the Midlands.

Chapter 15

Always Follow Your Intuition

by Yasmin Merchant

The power of intuition

Over the years, I've learned to follow my intuition. To me, intuition is when life's brush strokes touch and resonate with the inner depths of your soul, awakening your inner being. It's an inner knowing, a gut feeling beyond your ego, with no desire for attention or reward. It's a powerful inner driving force that sees past obstacles and leads you toward your true purpose. One such instance changed my life forever...

Finding a soul sister

One day, I came across a piece of written work that resonated deeply with me. As I read the words, it felt like the author spoke directly to my soul. *'Why do her words touch me so deeply?'* I wondered. I felt a strong urge to meet the author. I knew I had to attend when I saw the announcement for her book launch. Trusting my intuition, I went and met Paramjit in person. She turned out to be a soul sister. Our ten-year friendship is a testament to the power of intuition.

The universe offers us a helping hand through intuition, showing us signposts, like the book launch where I met Paramjit. Our connection was immediate, and our friendship has since blossomed into a decade-long journey of shared wisdom. Had I ignored that inner voice, it would have led to repeated frustration until I finally listened. When we met, it was as if we had known each other for lifetimes. *"Your words resonate with me,"* I told her. *"I feel the same,"* she replied and thus began the friendship that has enriched my life in countless ways.

Transformative friendship

A new world opened before me as I learned and grew through shared experiences and opportunities. Let me tell you more about this author: she is a retired university lecturer, a wise and inspiring lady, a carer and a compassionate friend. My life is more prosperous, and it's as though I have always known her. We have collaborated on projects, exchanging skills using the bartering system of old.

This golden thread of friendship has created a sanctuary for ladies 'of a certain age' living in communion. Over the years, we have become travel buddies, attended various evening and motivational classes, and discussed books and theatre. We have woven wonderful threads into the rich tapestry of a mutually sustaining, lifelong friendship. Following my intuition answered my yearning for a richer, more interesting life.

Wisdom from the elderly

Meeting Paramjit's dad reaffirmed the importance of caring for our parents. During our conversation, his wisdom came without prompting, lifting a heavy burden from my shoulders. He shared these wise words with me: *"Always remember to treat people well and respectfully and never hurt their feelings. Helping them in their time of need will bring the same returns to you."*

I enjoyed listening as he recounted how a former employee recognised him years later and helped him out of a tight spot. It reminded me that intuition often leads us to those who impart crucial life lessons. His advice resolved the issues weighing on my mind that day. It taught me to consult with and seek wisdom from at least one older person to gain insight into a dilemma I may be facing.

Life's grand stage

We are like animated puppets living out a play on this earthly stage. We are here to fine-tune our lives, polishing our characters' and souls' qualities and attributes. Teachers, healers, and elders are mapped out on our journey, imparting their gifts at the right time when we pay attention to our inner guidance.

Vehicles of expression

Since becoming a carer, I have learnt many valuable lessons. One enduring thread that guides me is never to judge another by appearance or intellect until you know their circumstances. I have a hidden handicap myself due to dyspraxia, which has made self-expression challenging and caused much frustration and tears. That changed when I discovered creative writing. My curiosity led me to follow another hunch. As before, seeing the words *"creative writing"* called to my innermost being as I searched a list of retreats available to carers. An entirely new avenue opened for me.

Knowing another form of self-expression is available to me is like a key to unlocking my distress and annoyance. It has become a tool that allows me to work through my feelings and better express my needs to the continuing care service. I can now hand over a diary that outlines the day-to-day needs of my elderly mother without feeling overcome with frustration and anxiety and daunted at the prospect of future meetings. Paying attention to my feelings and following my instincts around creative writing has proved so worthwhile. Once more, the solution to my burdens has unfolded beautifully.

Emotional mastery

Having been a carer for over 20 years, I have learnt another vital lesson – never act on your emotions until they have subsided. Once you enter calmer waters, it allows you to consider others' feelings, thoughts and circumstances before making hasty decisions. I have discovered this wisdom through my relationship with various carers over the years. No two people meet randomly. Nowadays, I realise that the people who show up in our lives do so for a reason. That reason is often a lesson that you need to learn from them to help you grow. After the lesson has been learned, the frustrations you experienced tend to disappear along with the person who caused them.

It may be pre-arranged for people to come into our lives. They undertake their role as our angels, our saving grace as we walk toward our soul growth. Once the source of your recent learning has left your life, along comes another random meeting to continue the journey of refining that old soul of yours.

Whenever I ask myself, *"What are these people doing in my life?"* My soul answers: *"They are pressing the buttons that challenge you the most, chiselling away to develop soul growth to perfection."*

Soul growth and harmony

Over the years, I have faced and overcome many challenges while caring for someone in partnership with others. Life has taught me to look at the bigger picture and consider the welfare of everyone involved, including those employed within my care. My daily life goal is to live in harmony and create a sanctuary for those in my care and the carers who come into my environment.

Imagine the joy of creating your little heaven in the corner of the earth where you abide, having learnt from your own mistakes. Taking a bird's eye view of life helps you to see things from an entirely different angle, bringing a new perspective. One of gratitude and fairness, where everyone wins. When faced with difficult choices, it sometimes helps to think it is better the devil you know. Take time to consider what is working well in the crucial areas of your situation. Do you need to risk negatively affecting someone else's income or livelihood by your actions?

I realised that whilst the agency could be slacking, I also need to stop and ask myself, *"Does the client and the carer need to suffer?"* In hindsight, I can now ask myself a series of questions when making a change that helps me clarify my decisions. I ask: *"Were my reasons for my actions sufficient to affect another's life? Have I applied fairness and honesty? Have I treated others how I would like to have been treated?"*

Remembering what makes your heart sing

I have many examples of how being attentive to your inner being is vital in moving forward. One of Derby's oldest department stores always delighted my daughter Tasha. She would sing with joy to visit it. It is a magical place, feeling like stepping into another world. We would find it very hard to leave this Aladdin's cave. Imagine the allure of each department, enticing you from one to the next: Russian dolls, Vintage Teddy bears, luxurious chocolates, an array of jewellery and accessories galore. A rainbow of colourful perfume bottles cleverly sited next to neon, pastel and bright nail polish, in turn, contrasted against a palate of makeup, branded hand and face creams.

Moving through the departments, we entered a living room displaying the finest wallpaper, paintings, upholstery, beautiful cushions, and tasteful ornaments. The mesmerising colours impress your senses, drawing you in, while continental gift packages evoke curiosity. Tasha was greatly interested in the art of sourcing such pieces and the skill of merchandising. She dreamed that one day, she would be part of this magical world.

Fast-forward to autumn, a time after Tasha achieved her degree when she searched for a buyer's assistant job near home.

Following the heart

In the simplest, most intuitive way, a heart can inspire the mind to express one's passion. Out of the blue, Tasha's heart led her to email the manager of the magnificent store, expressing her interest in working there. Her face broke into an enormous Cheshire-cat-like smile when she received an interview invitation.

"You have been fortunate in securing a place when a vacancy hasn't been advertised. How did you know to apply?" a colleague asked as she commenced employment. I could join her in answering: It's following that still, small voice, the spontaneous first thought that has etched a significant impression upon your heart. Once you remember the song you have come here to sing and stay open to intuition, the universe isn't far behind in conspiring to give birth to your dream.

Divine intervention

Significant moments of intuition have guided me in unexpected ways. For example, I searched for the gas board number in a dream. This vivid dream nudged me to investigate a gas leak in my home, potentially saving our lives. This experience again left me in awe of how intuition can manifest unexpectedly.

On another occasion, arriving at a hotel lobby in Edinburgh, I decided to go for a browse around town. The crafty cab driver we hailed drove us far beyond our destination, only to drop us in town literally seconds from the hotel! As we walked through town, I held an inner conversation about the injustice of it all.

Suddenly, I witnessed a £10 note swirling in the wind past the tourists ahead, only to flutter down, landing unexpectedly in my hands. This strengthened my knowledge that I am not the only witness to my thoughts; it's as though it's a two-way process when your heart is open, with a powerful force watching over you. This reinforced my trust that when you obey your intuition's guidance, it pays dividends.

I will leave you with one last golden thread of the intuition that increasingly weaves its magic in my life. In this instance, my daughter popped to the hairdressers in the village. After having her hair done, she discovered she had left her debit card and purse at home. Afraid of how the hairdresser would react and feeling embarrassed in front of other customers, she was greeted with: *"It's all been paid for; there's nothing left to pay."* When she arrived home, she was overwhelmed to learn that as I sat waiting for her, I had decided to surprise her by paying the hairdresser as a treat.

These experiences taught me to trust my intuition and embrace the magic it brings to my life. I connect to a higher force by following that inner voice, guiding me toward kindness, compassion, and love. Living intuitively makes life truly magical.

About Yasmin

Yasmin Merchant is a carer and hospital receptionist. She enjoys gardening, reading, creative writing, art, visiting places of interest, and holistic activities. She is also a trained reflexologist and a Reiki practitioner.

Conclusion

I hope that you have enjoyed reading this book and feel inspired by the stories within it. If so, we would love you to leave an honest review on Amazon.

Remember, should you find yourself doubting yourself at any point going forward, you can revisit one or more of these stories. This will remind you that we all face challenges, and we can all face our challenges and come out the other side stronger and wiser.

It is our sincere hope that you will take the time to pause and reflect on your own life, and to do what women often forget to do – celebrate your successes!

Celebration

by Sue Williams

Too often we forget to celebrate.
We go about our tasks, move from one to the next,
Become irate, frazzled, suddenly vexed,
Perhaps it's because we left it too late to celebrate.

To achieve takes time. There is reason in the rhyme,
Rhyme in our reason. Constant as the changing season,
Life moves on. Little time to revisit, ponder on, how creative
Flow addresses, those intricacies, our successes.

Stand back, admire the view, as artist purveys
Oil-fuelled hue. Gaze anew, in awe and wonder,
At the brush strokes fine, reflected shine of golden gown.
I dare you, smile, appreciate, disown that jaundiced frown.

Celebrate with pride. Before you resurrect your easel,
Pick up your fork, garnish your glass; "pop" goes the weasel!
Dance, rejoice, shout and sing, invite your friends to join right in.
It's in the celebration of our gifts that the wisest truly win!

Further Books and Resources

"The Believe You Can" **collaborative book series:**

Containing true life stories, poems and exercises aimed at supporting women facing life challenges:

- Believe You Can Succeed
- The Believe You Can Journal
- Believe You Can Face Your Fears and Confidently Claim the Life You Desire
- Believe You Can Live a Life You Love at 50+

- I Am Unique. Poems to Inspire Self-Belief

You can purchase all books from Amazon or via Sue's website: **www.sue-williams.com/books**

The Believe Oracle Cards

The Believe Oracle cards are a simple and effective way of getting to know yourself and learn how to overcome challenges you may face. These uplifting cards will help you tune into your authentic self and take action to achieve your dreams!

You can use the cards at: **www.sue-williams.com/app**

Printed in Great Britain
by Amazon